MODERN DRUMMER® *Legends*

Alex Van Halen

Modern Drummer Publisher/CEO **David Frangioni**

Managing Director/SVP **David Hakim**

Editorial Director **Adam Budofsky**

Managing Editor **Michael Dawson**

Art Director; Layout and Design **Scott Bienstock**

Music Transcription **Terry Branam**

Front cover photo by John Douglas
Back Cover photo by Christopher Otazo

Published by:
Modern Drummer Publications, Inc.
315 Ridgedale Ave #478
East Hanover, NJ 07936

Contents

Rick Malkin

Bottoms Up

Alex Van Halen's place in the pantheon of rock 'n' roll drummers is legendary. The incredible body of work that he created alongside his brother Eddie is memorialized in Van Halen's historic catalog of genre-defining music. With each new album, the group, which initially also featured bassist Michael Anthony and vocalist David Lee Roth, further developed its unique brand of music. Since Day 1, the foundation of that sound was the bottomless rumble and stratospheric crack of Alex Van Halen's drumming.

Though informed by the heaviest of classic rock's first-generation bands, from the outset Van Halen also had an ear to the future, retaining and even expanding their popularity in the midst of the new wave era, when they unabashedly incorporated keyboard hooks yet never betrayed their hard-rock base. Alex, like Eddie a self-described "tone chaser," was deeply invested in keeping the VH sound contemporary and exploratory, imbuing his drum performances not only with gargantuan beats and blazing fills, but captivating and idiosyncratic tones.

As much as any drummer in the history of rock, Alex Van Halen helped define the signature sound of his band—which is all the more startling given the fact that his guitar-playing brother is among *the* most influential players in the history of the music. Alex's energetic and unpredictable playing style and the unique bark of his sonic attack add an air of excitement to the music, and set the stage for the band's larger-than-life persona. Blending many influences, such as big band swing, blues, early rock 'n' roll, and even African drumming, Alex chooses from a wide palette.

And as his playing evolved from album to album and tour to tour, so did Alex's setup. Usually going for higher-pitched toms and ultra-deep bass drums, he would often experiment with different gear and technology to bring something new to the table. Incorporating Rototoms, timbales, cowbells, tube drums, and electronics, Alex spares no expense when it comes to finding the right equipment to achieve the sounds that are in his head.

The combination of Alex's drumming and Eddie's trailblazing guitar wizardry has always been the symbiotic backbone of Van Halen. The band's lineup certainly experienced upheavals, most dramatically in the vocalist department. In 1985 David Lee Roth was replaced by Sammy Hagar, who fronted the band during several of its most successful albums and tours. Roth made a highly publicized reappearance with the band during the 1996 MTV Music Video Awards, but was soon replaced by Gary Cherone, who himself stepped aside after the *Van Halen III* album and tour to make room for the return of Hagar. Roth was back again in 2006, the same year that Michael Anthony's role was taken over by Eddie's son, Wolfgang.

Perhaps the most significant event in the recent history of the band, however, came in late 2020, with the passing of Eddie Van Halen. The compilation of this book, including *Modern Drummer*'s most recent interview with Alex Van Halen, was completed prior to the news of Eddie's passing. Given that the constant throughout all of Van Halen's achievements—and what guaranteed their stature not only on the charts but in popular culture—was the bloodline of the Van Halen brotherhood, this book can be viewed not only as a tribute to one of the greatest rock drummers of all time, but to the glorious music that Alex and Eddie created together.

by Terry Branam and Adam Budofskly

"Give Me Some Emotion!"
The 2020 Interview

by Ilya Stemkovsky

"This is a life, not a career, not just a job," says Alex Van Halen, emphatically. "This is what we do. It's a life." From the outside, Van Halen has always "kicked ass." The tales of girls and booze and drugs and infighting made the headlines, but the sound blasting out of the speakers when that needle dropped was always something very serious. It was a sound made by master craftsmen, each musician inspiring a generation of imitators who would form their own bands. But nothing ever really sounded like Van Halen, before or since.

That life Alex Van Halen references has been a long, often tumultuous roller coaster of a career spanning four decades filled with musical riches. Not the least of which was the surprising late-era triumph that was 2012's *A Different Kind of Truth*, the unlikely reunion studio effort with Diamond David Lee Roth back on vocal duty. In it, Roth croons and shrieks, Wolfgang Van Halen pumps the low end, Edward Van Halen does his inimitable thing, and Alex sounds like he's out to prove that it ain't over yet. The tours that followed confirmed what die-hards knew all along: that Van Halen was still mighty, and an older but wiser Alex Van Halen was still a force behind those tubs, out to inspire a new generation who might not have been around during the golden days. What a life it's been.

MD: Is the songwriting process any different today than it's been over the years?

Alex: Each song had to be a creative experience. That's how Ed and I approach it. Each song needs to be unique and have its own energy. You put everything into it and see what happens. All the people who think they know how the band operates, maybe even including Dave, weren't 100-percent there all the time. Ed and I are the only ones there day and night. When they leave, Ed and I go back in and work on shit. Or Ed, Wolf, and I go back in and work on it. And "working" means sometimes just playing it, or Ed finishing another piece of it. So when we get into the studio to actually record it, and there's some friction, it's easy to say, "The brothers are fighting again." [laughs] Being in a band is no different from any other territorial dispute. Everybody is trying to claim a certain piece of territory. The real solution is to play together, to play as a unit. You're much stronger that way. Conflict is good up to a certain point. Conflict causes friction, causes heat, but once it gets to a certain point, that's not good.

MD: So a little conflict is good for the music, but the outside noise doesn't really factor.

Alex: All these people are writing books about the band and they know nothing about the inner workings of this band. And Ed and I don't say anything because we're not in the business of bullshitting on the internet and books

and all that kind of crap. We just want to play. It's that simple.

MD: Is everyone always free to contribute?

Alex: Ed would come in with the licks and the band would put the music together, and we would make songs out of it. It was a very communal process. If you had a thought or idea, you'd just throw it in and the loudest voice wins. It was not a sterile, clinical approach. It was like a panel, very organic. That was something that was lacking as time went by. We would rehearse, and if we had it at about 80-percent right, that was the prime time to go into the studio. Leave enough room for error, leave enough room for spontaneity, leave enough room for God knows what. Because in those moments, the magic happens. There should be a percentage left undone. Maybe it's a Buddhist or Daoist thing, but never finish anything. In certain countries

asked if he ever went to school. And he said, "Hell no, if I ever went to school, I'd end up being a teacher." And teachers are wonderful and should get a halo for their job. But the point is, whoever teaches you, you're only going to learn what he did. But when Buddy Rich was asked who influenced him, he was very humble and said, "Everyone before me was my teacher." And that's exactly how music is. It's a larger, communal thing, not just isolated little things.

MD: How important was a producer in Van Halen world?

Alex: Part of it was the conflict between the band and Dave. One of the things that made everything work was that we came from opposite ends of the spectrum. Dave was vaudeville and he claimed to be James Brown. Ed and I were coming from Cream, Led Zeppelin, Black Sabbath. So having that strange chemistry is what made it work, oddly enough. But you do need a mediator.

MD: What do you think made the band excel onstage?

Alex: Van Halen is a live band. After we honed our skills, you learn the connection between the people and the music. Playing live, there should be no dead space. Never turn your back on the audience and never insult them. They are equal to you. That line that separates the audience from the stage, that's not a line. That's just to keep them from puking on your shit. [laughs] You're there to make the audience feel good.

MD: It has to be strange for you to see how different the consumption of recorded music is nowadays.

Alex: Modern technology sucks. There's nothing left in the music business. It's a bunch of ones and zeroes. In the old days, you'd get a dollar a record, and now you'll get fifty cents for 275,000 streams. It's insane. It's wrong. Now the only thing you have is playing live,

"The musical experience is not just

they don't finish a bottle of water; they always leave some behind. Always leave something unfinished.

MD: It sounds like the band still loves things that are unplanned.

Alex: One of the funniest things that Ed and I always laugh about is when he would do some break and it would completely fall apart, and at the end we'd all come together. We would say, "It sounds like you fell down the stairs but you landed on your feet." [laughs] The musical experience is not just the notes, not just the sound. It's the physicality, the spiritual aspect, everything rolled into one. Sometimes when you play, it all falls into place, and other times you say, "Man, what a strange night that was." Unfortunately, there's an undue burden that comes on the drummer to hold it together. When some of the other guys are not with it, you have to somehow stitch it together, if you can. Our dad used to say, "When the drums come in, the song should go to a new level." He never told me what that meant. [laughs]

MD: Maybe you just understood it instinctively.

Alex: It's not a rote repetition of what you learned in class. A classic thing I remember was when Buddy Rich was

Otherwise we would never have gotten anything done.

MD: But how loud was an outside voice? Your music and drumming seem very personal to your own thing.

Alex: It's the same thing with Ed, when he picks up a guitar. You can run it through all kinds of effects, but the essence is in the way you hit or touch the instrument. That's what makes it so personal. Ed can play my drums and he doesn't sound anything like me, and vice versa.

MD: Amazingly, you've never really played outside of Van Halen.

Alex: This is my band. I don't need to go elsewhere. Creatively, this is the place where it happens. This is the band that Ed and I started. Just like my loyalty to Ludwig, that will never change. My loyalty is to this band.

MD: Your Ludwig relationship goes way back.

Alex: In 1979, Tama wanted me to become an endorser and they wanted to give me a lot of money, and I said, "No, I play Ludwig. Thank you, goodbye." I had a relationship with Bill Ludwig III, who was a lovely guy. To me, personal relationships and inner connections are much more important than the other shit. It's the personal relations that last.

which is ironic, because that's how it all started.

MD: Did it matter who was singing? Did you feel your playing change?

Alex: Sammy has a great rhythmic sense and of course that voice. Dave was much more of a poet. Dave is creative. Ninety percent of it is garbage, but that ten percent is f**king worth it, man. What planet did you come from? And we grew up together.

MD: Would either of them suggest things to you?

Alex: If Dave came in with a song, I would respect how they heard it. And then it's the old trick, "Keep your friends close and your enemies closer." [laughs] And that means, "Okay, I'll listen to you, but then I'm gonna make it mine." And by the end of the process, it will sound nothing like what you hummed me. Dave would ask for me to do some "jungle" [referring to tom-heavy beats]. And I say, "Okay, Dave, you got it, whatever." [laughs] There was the African jungle, the South American jungle….

MD: One imagines that these relationships are why the music is so tight, for better or worse.

Alex: We were in the same bus, up to and including *1984*. The same bus! And that included the sound and light guys. Leonardo da Vinci said, "Large rooms distract the mind; small rooms focus the mind." When you're all tight in close quarters, it focuses your energies, and you learn how to deal with issues and problems. If you're in a large space, you never even have to say hello to the other guys. What's that all about? I'd rather have someone wake up in the morning and say, "Hey, f**k you!" as opposed to not saying anything at all. I'm serious. Give me some emotion! That's what this is about. Music is a celebration of being human. With the drums at the forefront! [laughs]

MD: You played with Michael Anthony for so long. Was there an adjustment to Wolfgang?

Alex: Wolf just happened to be in the studio when Ed and I were playing. He chimed in and I said, "That's a nice groove he's got going. Who is that?" There was a curtain and I couldn't see

but they never made it to a record, so now was the time to do it. And if we didn't all agree, we certainly would not have done it. From a performance standpoint, it's more geared to looking at the totality of the song, instead of, "Look how bitchin' I'm playing this." Ed and I are very aware of what makes a song work or not. After you play a song a thousand times, after a while you don't think anymore. Something else comes out. Ed and I used to go into the studio, and we would play literally for *days*. And something would come up, sometimes good, and sometimes not good.

MD: And the recording process was similar?

Alex: I love Les Paul, but man, he really hurt the recording process by inventing the multitrack. The concept of recording everything with nine hundred microphones in their own little area and putting it all back together as if it was one or two microphones…I've got

meantime—maybe we've gotten worse. It doesn't make a difference to us. We're going to give you the best that we got, right now. And I think the audience senses that. But there were some [older recordings] that I wasn't happy with, but what are you going to do? It's there. [laughs]

MD: Do you have any sagely advice about practicing versus playing live?

Alex: Practicing is a solitary endeavor. You have to do it alone. Nobody's seeing you and it goes unrewarded. But when you're there to share your music with people, you play it. Don't work it, just play. Don't overthink it. The overthinking happens when you're practicing. When you're there at the gig, just play. We've all gone through this. You want to be the best you can be, and the harder you try, the worse you f**k up, and it doesn't happen for you. I've read many interviews, like with Dave Weckl, and they all say the same thing.

the notes, not just the sound. It's the physicality, the spiritual aspect, everything rolled into one."

who it was, and it was Wolf. One thing led to another, and we all thought it was a big risk to take, but Wolf stepped up to the plate by being respectful of the parts that Mikey played. He didn't trash them, and it was a very mature choice for him to play the parts as they were on the record, but with a little bit of movement. But the second thing I told him after "Great job" was "Stay the f**k off my drums." [laughs]

MD: Talk about the songs that made up *A Different Kind of Truth*.

Alex: We didn't use entire [older] songs but the D.N.A. of what we felt propels the band. Van Halen is not just a one-dimensional band. It was very insightful of Dave to make a socio-political comment on a song like "China Town," that everything is made in China now. All of this is a tangential conversation about where we live and how we live. Music is not an isolated event. We are the same as the people we play for, and we're just making observations. And some of the songs were redone

news for you, why don't you just record it using two microphones? Drums don't make the sound an inch away from the drumhead. Drums need to uncork and breathe and [mix with] the sound of the room. It's phenomenal how Led Zeppelin did that. They were very aware of that. They were probably one of the few bands that were old-school for the way stuff was recorded. The delay of the room, all those things. It's a lost art. And the sound that you make is as personal as anything else. A vocalist has his sound and an instrumentalist has his.

MD: Do you ever feel tied into beats and fills you wrote decades ago?

Alex: The band looks at it like we're there to serve the audience. And because [the latest tour] was a deep-cut tour, we played songs we hadn't touched in thirty years. And they were kind of fresh. It was nice. And you don't want to completely demolish what you'd done by overplaying or show how good you've gotten in the meantime. Or maybe we haven't gotten good in the

Once you relax into it, it's going to be great. Just play.

MD: Sounds like that has served you well.

Alex: We spent the first thirty years of our lives trying to cloud what reality was, and you have a different interpretation of it. [laughs] But by the time you're thirty, you'd better change your ways or you ain't gonna make it any further. I believe we're very lucky to be able to do this, to make music, and make a living at it, and to share it with people. We're very lucky, so don't f**k it up. That's the message. When our dad passed away, after our long life of touring and making music, and yeah there was alcohol involved, but I looked at him, and unspoken, I said, "I'll try to make it better." So I quit. You do have an obligation and responsibility to [work] without artificial inspiration. We all look for some kind of meaning in life, but Ed and I were lucky that we found it early. So I can't complain.

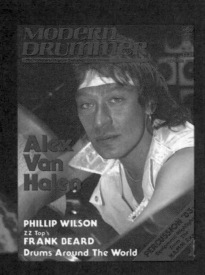

"You *Play* Music, You Don't Work It."
The 1983 Interview

Alex Van Halen's debut on the cover of *Modern Drummer*, in October 1983, came at a time when the band had inarguably hit its stride as bona fide arena-rock headliners. Two solid years of touring behind their fourth and fifth albums, *Fair Warning* and *Diver Down*, saw Alex, Eddie, singer David Lee Roth, and bassist Michael Anthony playing multi-night engagements in the biggest cities of North and South America, and enjoying massive airplay with hit covers of Martha and the Vandellas'"Dancing in the Street" and "Roy Orbison's "Oh, Pretty Woman." Little did any of us know that Van Halen's *biggest* successes were still to come, with December's release of the single "Jump" and January's blockbuster *1984* album and its classic cuts "Panama," "I'll Wait," and "Hot for Teacher." But in '83 Alex and company were definitely already feeling their oats as one of the hottest tickets in rock, true rock originals who celebrated their own commercial success and widespread adulation with gusto.

MD: Who were some of your influences growing up?

Alex: I started playing drums when I heard the Dave Clark Five and when I saw Ringo getting all the girls in the Beatles movie. He wasn't exactly the handsomest-looking guy, but I figured that if drums could do that for him, I'd give it a shot. Also, we always did have a very heavy musical thing happening. I started out on piano and went through violin, clarinet, saxophone—you name it, I tried it. I played guitar for about a year, and I had some classical training—flamenco and reading.

At the same time, Edward had bought a drumset. To pay for the drums, he had to sell newspapers, and while he was out selling newspapers, I'd chuck the guitar and get on the drums, and it was great. Ed would come back, and he'd play drums and I'd play guitar. Finally he just realized that we should switch instruments because I could play drums much better than he could. So he picked up the guitar and I could just tell by the way he was moving his fingers around that he could do things that I would never be able to do, no matter how hard I practiced. I guess we were right.

MD: How long did you take piano lessons?

Alex: For ten or fifteen years. The drums were kind of secondary at that point, more like recreation and a good time to get together with the guys at about twelve, thirteen years old. That was the fun aspect. The work part was practicing piano, because the teacher we had was a concert pianist. At that time we didn't have a whole lot of money, and it got to the point where he said, "Look, I'm not even going to charge you kids. You just come here and you practice and you play, because I think you have talent." Our teacher thought that we had something and was kind of disappointed when we said we didn't want to play piano anymore, at least full time.

MD: When did you finally realize drums was what you wanted to do and it was no longer just recreational?

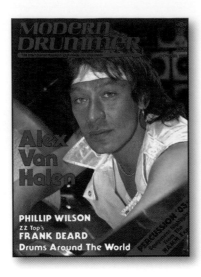

Alex: I think it just happened very gradually, because by the time I was thirteen, I was working in clubs with my dad, who was a professional musician. They let me sit in and my dad said, "Just keep your head down and nobody will notice that you're only thirteen."

MD: What kind of music were you playing?

Alex: Jazz. And later on to make a few bucks on the side when the rock thing wasn't happening for us, I worked with my dad doing weddings. Bar mitzvahs, parties. And this is where you play everything. You play Latin stuff, you play jazz, they tried to play rock 'n' roll, but with an accordion and a saxophone it's a bit difficult.

Finally I made enough money where I could quit the other job I had. We're moving along about five years now. At that point, I was working in a machine shop and working at night playing with the rock band. It was Edward and me, always with two other guys. When we weren't making money doing that, I'd play with my dad. Finally, when the four of us got together and we started working, I slowly phased out the bar mitzvah stuff and the stuff with my dad.

MD: There was a quote from Eddie that said you were doing odd-time stuff when you were really young.

Alex: Yeah, we messed around with it. It's interesting. At a certain point you have to decide whether you're going to play for musicians, for yourself, or for the audience. Ninety-nine percent of the people do not understand music. They don't have any training and they don't go to school to learn the stuff, so why bore them with it? If you want to put out a special album that sounds like…well…I don't want to name any names. But go ahead and do it, just don't expect to make a living off it and don't be upset.

You know, it's funny, you get these people who write this way-out music that nobody really understands, including the artist, and they're always saying how they're not interested in

record sales. But yet when the album is a flop, they say, "Hey, what's the matter with you people? Can't you understand that I've created some art here?" I wish they'd make up their minds.

MD: Do you think the classical orientation affected your musicality as a youngster at all?

Alex: I think the classical aspect was only just to gain the groundwork, the actual foundation of music, and to understand how it's put together and what makes it work. Being able to read music obviously helps. It just gave us so much more insight into what's really going on. Then you can take a Beatles song and tear it apart and know how it works, so you can steal it and write your own Beatles song. [laughs] It's definitely a help. I'm not saying we should play classical music, but the basic training was great for us.

MD: What about formal training on drums? Did you have any?

Alex: None. Formal training to me seems like a strange word. Just because you pay somebody, does that mean it's formal training? I've hung around different drummers and they've said, "Hey, try this," or "You're doing this wrong," but as far as going to a school and doing X amount of hours of classwork a day and paying up the butt for it, no, I didn't do that. I gave up on the "formal" lessons after the piano.

MD: So how did you teach yourself?

Alex: Just by listening and by working. When I finally started playing drums full-time—which was about when I was eighteen—we were playing all the clubs. To be able to work those clubs, you had to be able to play every song that existed, so aside from learning how to arrange songs—anything from James Brown to Led Zeppelin to the Doobie Brothers—with only bass, drums, guitar, and vocal, you had to really manipulate things. That's partially how Van Halen got such a fat sound out of such a small group.

MD: I read that when you were in high school, you arranged a production of *West Side Story* for a fifteen-piece jazz ensemble.

Alex: Yeah, it was junior college, and it was a major flop.

MD: Where did the arranging knowledge come from?

Alex: I went to school for that. I would have had a degree in music, but I quit after a while because I just wasn't getting anything out of it. It got to a certain point where these intellectuals—and I'm not knocking any intellectuals—would, just for the sake of making a song interesting in their eyes, go through a meter change or a key change for no reason at all. Song-wise, structurally, the song didn't hold up. Meanwhile, the four of us were writing songs in typical I-IV-V, just

ear to be able to tell you, "Well, wait a minute guys, you're going overboard on this section. Let's cool it." And then other times, it may need a little extra this or that. That's why I think a lot of bands who are producing themselves are digging a hole for themselves. If you spend twenty-four hours straight on a certain part, there is no way in hell that you're going to leave that off

do now onstage for five hours a night. So for us, this is a vacation. Two hours onstage, no prob. So they'd say, "Get yourself a job. Look at your cousin— he's an accountant."

MD: Generally parents who have been in the profession go one of two ways. They either really support it or they say, "Learn from my mistakes—I've seen it and it can break your heart."

Rick Malkin

simple stuff with a memorable melody. Then these guys would say, "You guys are musical prostitutes. You're writing garbage." At that point, I said, "Alright, I'll take my garbage and peddle it elsewhere."

I don't hold any grudges, but I think they're very closed-minded. Count Basie said, "If it sounds good, it is good." If it takes more to get it across, fine. If it takes less, fine. That's where the producer comes in. He has the

the record. It's going to get in there somehow, and it takes that producer to say, "Forget it. It doesn't work."

MD: Were your parents always supportive of music as a career?

Alex: As a career, no. It was always, "Get yourself a job," while we'd be busting our chops playing five or six hours in an evening—five forty-five-minute sets. And we weren't doing what most club bands do, which is just stand there and play. We'd do the show that we

Alex: That's the same thing my dad would have said, but he was always gone working, so he didn't really have the chance. It was a typical story. We went out and played and played and played. Sure we didn't have any money, and sure this broke down, and sure there were lousy people we had to work with, such as pseudo managers and club owners. But the audiences were always there, and it was a great time. Some people call it paying your

dues, but we just called it having fun. We had a good time. I wouldn't have wanted it any different.

MD: Has anything changed now that you're on a bigger scale? Was any of the magic lost?

Alex: No, not at all.

MD: Even the intimacy of the club as opposed to a large hall?

Alex: No, not really. It's just on a large scale. I think some people tend to put a barrier between themselves and the audience. I don't know why they do that, but we try to keep in touch.

MD: You have a reputation for being a hardy partier. How does one maintain that kind of pace and keep the gig intact?

Alex: Rock 'n' roll is a lifestyle. It's a thing where there are no rules. You can play what you want, you can wear what you want, and nobody tells you that you have to have one bass drum, one snare, one rack tom, and one floor tom. Even though Louie Bellson wasn't exactly a rock 'n' roller, he had the right attitude—you *play* the music, you don't *work* it, and you don't have to live by the rules. The whole thing of the lifestyle of not having any rules, includes—I hate to use the word "party," because then you think of Foghat—but I think all of Van Halen, including the entourage, are pretty much into having a good time. Of course, you don't want to spread yourself too thin, but as long as you can do the gig, it's okay.

MD: Have you learned a method by which to pace yourself during the show?

Alex: I think basically it's that you know you have to be there for two hours, and you know that those lights make the stage about 150 degrees, so you pace yourself. One consideration is the way the set is put together, as far as which songs are more difficult to play than others, where your drum solo is going to be, and when the guitar solo will be so you'll have a few minutes' rest. But I'll be honest with you, the actual

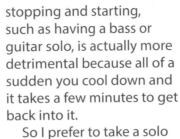

stopping and starting, such as having a bass or guitar solo, is actually more detrimental because all of a sudden you cool down and it takes a few minutes to get back into it.

So I prefer to take a solo out of the fastest song. And I don't solo too long. I just make it long enough to make it interesting, because I think a drummer's place is more in playing with the band and kicking them, as opposed to playing alone for twenty minutes. It's very admirable to see somebody who has practiced eight or ten hours a day, and see him do a fantabulous buzz roll, but again, the people don't understand. Twenty minutes just seems unreasonable to me—it's just a good time for the rest of the band members to take a break while the good old drummer is back there beating the hell out of the drums, indulgent, getting cardiac arrest. A lot of things that these drummers play could be done during a song, and it would make the songs much more interesting. I think it's an ego problem a lot of drummers have.

Drums not being a melodic instrument—even though there have been some things done to them where you can make them a little more melodic, such as the Simmons, the Octobans, and such—it's not

really a front-type instrument. At least that's my philosophy. I mean, being a drummer, I would appreciate having the drums out front, but I look at it from the standpoint of the average person who listens and whistles along with a song. He's not going to know a Swiss triplet from a flam. I don't want to spend my time doing something just to impress other drummers. It is true, though, that in rock 'n' roll, a drummer figures more prominently in a band than in previous styles. While I don't see the drummer as being up front, more attention is paid since there are usually only four people, so the sound *is* more important than in other styles.

MD: You have said that a concert

should be an event. How much consideration do you give towards showmanship?

Alex: Showmanship, first of all, should come naturally. It shouldn't be forced, and it only comes through constantly playing so that after a while, you're not even aware of it. When Buddy Rich plays, he's a showman. He looks great, and I don't think he consciously sits there and says, "Okay, now I gotta do this and do that." Nowadays I see a lot of people who really concentrate heavily on twirling their sticks, and so they drop one and miss a beat. A drummer can't move around too much. I mean, I've seen drummers who will get up on the drums, walk around, and it's very novel, very good and interesting. But I think it detracts from the music, which is, after all, the most important thing. It's important that it be a unit. It's fine to show off a drum thing here and there, or a guitar or a bass here and there, but the bottom line is that it has to be a unit.

MD: What is required of you as drummer for Van Halen? What is your role in that unit?

Alex: That's a complicated question because it works the same with the guitar and bass. Everything has to flow together; it has to go into a certain direction. There's a beginning, middle, and end of a song. If a guy were to do a solo during an entire song, it obviously wouldn't fit. It has to be what's musically appropriate, and yet,

in the quiet part? Nobody says it has to be right there. You can't slow down while the other guys are still speeding up, but just flow with the songs; flow with the other musicians.

MD: Do you subscribe at all to the bass/drummer relationship theory? It seems like you play off the guitar.

Alex: I don't think the bass/drummer thing makes any sense at all. Obviously, there's an underlying pattern that the bass and the drums play, but as far as throwing in extra stuff or doing fills, I think it's much more interesting to play along with the guitar. Again, when you're in the studio, you're a little bit limited as far as the freedom of really going hog wild and taking a big

Alex: Yeah, a lot. Especially when you're on the road for eight months. At first it starts out basically by the rules, but after a while we'll just do a set completely backwards, or sideways, or we'll throw in a song at the last moment for no reason at all. We opened for the Stones in '81. There were about 100,000 people there, and we had the set all written out, what we were going to play and how the segues were going to be. In the middle, Dave just said, "Wait, wait, wait—let's play 'Summertime Blues.'" So we played "Summertime Blues." What the hell.

MD: What is your approach to a new tune?

Alex: Usually Ed comes up with the

Rick Malkin

at the same time, you try to throw in something that's a little bit different—something you may have heard or seen some other person do or maybe something that came to you in the middle of a dream.

I think the most important thing is to let it flow. If you worry about it too much, then it does sound mechanical. The first priority for a drummer is to keep the meter, and if you really start worrying about that, then often it's not happening. I'm sure all drummers can relate to that. That's why they have click tracks in the studios. Ted [Templeman, producer] will not allow a click track. It's got to be there naturally, and that's the way it goes. And I agree. I think that's what music is—music flows. So what if it slows down a little

chance, because you've got that one take and it's the pure thing. You can edit it and try this here, but that's all tape magic. Live, I think I play a little bit different. I play more open—more stuff that I would normally not do in the studio—because when you're making a song, don't forget, you have to live with that thing for the rest of your life.

MD: When you go offstage, you can say, "Well, tomorrow night I can do that part a little bit better."

Alex: And not just better or worse, but something that might not be appropriate, that might not fit. And again, Ed might not always play the same thing, but that's the beauty of live.

MD: Is there a lot of improvisation onstage?

music and then he'll have a certain idea in mind as to how he would like to hear the percussion. So he'll say, "Why don't you try it this way," and usually it's by name—"Play it à la so-and-so." And sure, I'll listen to it.

MD: Who are some of the so-and-sos?

Alex: [laughs] Well, everybody has a little different style. If I listen to Steve Smith for a couple of days, then for a couple of days I'll play just like him, just to get the feel of it. If I listen to Bonham, I'll sound like him. It's really a chameleon-type thing. When we do a new song, I'll play it a certain way, but the next day, I will have listened to somebody else and I'll play it a little bit different. All of a sudden, in the middle of the song, somebody will say, "Hey, hold on a second. The song sounds different. What's the matter?" I'll just keep my mouth shut.

I think it's beneficial to listen to any and all different [types of] drumming. Not everybody is an originator. Things have been rehashed and rehashed over and over, and you can build on that. For instance, nowadays, when you turn on the radio, almost every single drum sound is identical to the next. There are very few drummers where you can actually hear the difference. I think it's the multitude of different influences that you can finally hone down, and you filter through what you like and apply it to the song that makes it happen.

MD: Sometimes you adopt different styles from different people, and

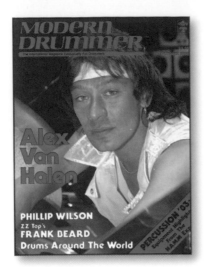

MD: Is that where it ends?
Alex: [laughs] That's it. I like the old ones such as the old Dave Clark Five. It's a great sound for those days, with one overhead.
MD: I wonder if that's why it sounded so great.
Alex: Yeah. Lately, now that we have a new studio we're working in, we can try some different stuff, like different miking techniques. It's amazing, everybody has his own technique for miking drums, from what kind of mics to use, to the placement, to the room, to whether the drummer should be isolated, to whether the other musicians are in the same room as the amplifiers, to temperature control—all of which really makes a difference.

able to mess around since Edward built a studio.
MD: Is the writing really a democratic process? All the records say, "Composed by Van Halen."
Alex: That's because we didn't want to lock ourselves into the problems other bands have, which are, "I wrote this word and you wrote that word and I wrote this guitar lick…." Basically, the music is written by Ed and the lyrics are written by Dave, but by the time it's actually on vinyl, it's essentially a four-way deal. That also includes the stage setup, the way it looks, and the songs we're going to play. It encompasses the entire thing.
MD: Where did the idea for "Big Bad Bill" come from?
Alex: Dave had just bought one of those new portable radios with the little tape recorder. He was testing it at home and picked up this program from, believe it or not, Cincinnati, and it was some kind of weird '40s-type hour. He taped it and we heard the song and

"At a certain point you have to decide

suddenly you've developed your own style because you've made your own.
Alex: Sure. A lot of it comes subconsciously. You don't even know you're doing it. I think a drummer's sound is as important as the way he plays. A lot of times I can recognize a drummer right off the bat by a certain sound he has. I think the drum sound is his signature, and I can usually tell who's who just by the sound. A lot of times I'm not in agreement with some of the sounds. Russ Kunkel is a great drummer, but I can't stand his snare sound. Sorry, Russ. My personal taste is a little more live sound, such as Bonham's snare sound. I like Neil Peart's tom sound, but not his kicks and his snare. Don't get me wrong, though. Anybody who spends his lifetime devoted to music—the suffering, the discipline, and all that—is to be commended. But I have different tastes from other people. Bill Bruford is a great player, but again, I can't stand his snare sound. Usually the snare sound is the signature of the drummer.
MD: Whose do you like?
Alex: Bonham's.

"Sunday Afternoon in the Park" was done with one overhead, one remote—which means the other microphone was at the other end of the room—and that was basically it. The band was in the room, and that's why you hear the synthesizer along with the drums. The vibration got picked up by the synthesizer. It was a mistake, but we left it on the record.
MD: You guys don't do a lot of overdubbing.
Alex: No. There's no sense to it. We go in and cut the song once or twice and if it's not happening, we move on to something else, because then the magic is lost. If you do it too many times, it gets stale. I recently read an article in *Modern Drummer* about somebody saying you edit the tape, take a little piece from here and put it over here, and take the best takes of the two and put it together, and that way everybody's happy. *Bullshit!* The person who played that knows that he didn't play it all the way through, which to me doesn't make any sense. Get it right. If not, go back and practice it. Luckily now we have the time to be

it just seemed to click. So we set it up like the old days, with one microphone in the room, no separation, no vocal booths, no nothing, played it, and there it was—one take.
MD: I'm assuming that when you were younger you messed around with brushes. But when was the last time you had seriously played with them?
Alex: That took a couple days of brushing up—ha, ha, ha. It took a couple of days just to get the feel of it again, but basically, if you've done it once, it's like riding a bicycle. I'm no profound brush player, but it fit the song and we said, "Let's go for it."

But I know, you're saying, "Who would think a hard rock band would play 'Big Bad Bill' or 'Happy Trails'?" A sense of humor is very important. If you take yourself too seriously, you find out that you're in the wrong thing. Like I said earlier, you *play* music, you don't *work* it; you don't *compete* it. Just let it flow. It's there for the enjoyment. Not for, "Hey, I'm better than you," or "I can play faster than you." I think that's really a deterrent to young musicians. A lot of times they give up before they really start because they say, "I can't play that fast or do that." Who says you have to play like this guy? It's really a shame, because I've heard a lot of good music and raw talent.

MD: That goes back to something that Eddie said in an article about how there is no consideration to the "right way" to do something. He just does what feels right.

Alex: There isn't. And now all of a sudden people look at Ed and say, "Wow, that's amazing. Why didn't I think of that?" There's nothing wrong with experimenting and trying different things.

MD: On a cover tune, is there any consideration given to how it was originally played?

Alex: Sometimes, but mostly not. First of all, let me say that a lot of people knock us for doing covers. You get the record reviews and they say, "Van Halen is really coming to a creative dead end, because they now have three cover tunes on their record." If you take the

we'll do the old technique, one overhead and maybe, just to cover me, we'll put a couple in the bass drums and some close up for the toms. Usually in the studio I record with single heads for the reason of isolation. That way you get a purer tone. The purists will say, "The drum can't resonate unless it has both heads on it," and that routine. The snare is just miked from the top, and lately what we've done is put the mic right against the shell. I'm using a rosewood snare [6.5x14] now, and that's how I got the sound on "Pretty Woman," which gets a much more live sound. I always record with the kit on a wood [surface], with wood around it, so it does bounce around a little bit. If you hear the echo, most of it is acoustic, not machine. It makes a difference. I like to keep it generic.

MD: What kind of heads do you use?

Alex: CS black dot. I don't like to switch between the studio and live setups because then it sounds different.

the need for all that stuff, saying you can do it on one tom, one kick, and a snare.

Alex: I've heard that argument, and I agree and I disagree. When you have a simple setup, it forces you to be a little more creative. But I think if you don't have the discipline to be creative anyway, why bother with even a simple setup? Why not go super simple? I admit, a lot of people will take advantage of having the toms, and all they do are tom rolls. When, you're right, you can play a lot of different patterns and interesting things just on one rack and one floor. Back to Bonham—he did it.

The advantage of a large set, obviously, is that you have much more of a tonal range. If you can be creative on a four-piece set, and then augment it with different intonations and different sounding drums, such as Rototoms or the Simmons or a double kick or even a second snare to have a floppy snare sound like Russ Kunkel,

whether you're going to play for musicians, for yourself, or for the audience."

singing off of "Dancing in the Streets," it's nowhere near the song. We could have very easily just bent the lyrical content, bent the melody just a little bit, and made another song, but we felt that was a song we wanted to go for. Plus we felt that Martha and the Vandellas could use the royalties to buy some new lipstick. But this goes back to the same thing: if it sounds good, it *is* good. The old philosophy we have is that if a song is a good song, it remains good. You have to realize that Elvis Presley rarely wrote his own songs, and neither did the Beatles when they first started.

MD: You explained how you recorded the drums on "Sunday Afternoon in the Park." Obviously you don't record like that all the time; is there a general rule of thumb?

Alex: Well, that's the whole point—there is no standard thing. Sometimes

I know the acoustical problems of the live situation as opposed to the controlled studio situation, but to me it seems like if this is the drum you recorded it on, then play it that way live.

MD: Doesn't your setup alter with the situation, though?

Alex: No.

MD: Most people with large setups live don't end up recording with them.

Alex: If the song requires only kick, snare, and a couple of tom fills, why strip it down? I feel comfortable with what I play. I know where everything is, so why mess with it?

MD: So you feel that you don't always have to use all of it?

Alex: Of course not. Just because it's all there, it doesn't mean you have to smack everything the whole time.

MD: There are a lot of pros and cons to large setups. A lot of "purists" criticize

then I think it can definitely be a plus. Having a large setup, though, should not be an excuse for just rolling down the toms. I think a lot of people cover their butts by having a large set and doing that kind of tom fill. It can work both ways, but a large set can give you so many more possibilities and angles to work from. It shouldn't be used as a crutch, though.

MD: In a lot of what I've read about Van Halen, there is a feeling, which David has even outwardly said, that the band does not take its music seriously. How do you interpret that statement, and where do you draw the line between not taking the music seriously, yet taking your playing seriously?

Alex: What Dave meant by that is that we don't write songs that change the course of history. We don't go into outer space, we don't use double entendres, and we don't get into politics. It's more of a reflection of what we see around us—our experiences. Fortunately there have been enough people who've had the same experiences, so they can relate to it.

MD: He made the comment that there are even times that he doesn't care whether he remembers the right words.

Alex: The bottom line, obviously, is that the music has to be there. By saying "not too seriously," we just mean that we take it as it comes. If tomorrow the whole album takes a dive, then what the hell, we'll record another one. I just think that a lot of people take it too seriously when they get up onstage—they're out to change the course of history and they get so serious that they go off the deep end. If you can take it with a smile, great.

It should really be *you* up there.

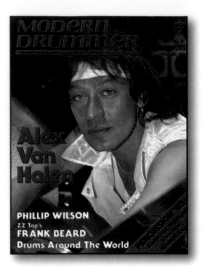

longer kick drum. I wasn't really happy with the sound I was getting, so I tried a longer bass drum and it really did make a difference. Each one is a regular 14x26, and when you join both of them together, it's 28x26. That's my right one. The left one is a 28x24 and then on the outside of each of those, I have a 14x24. I may end up only using three, because that right bass drum sounds good by itself. The center drums are open; there are no heads on them. They're all miked, and what happens is I get a balance between a double-headed drum and a single-headed one because the air goes through the pipe and forces air into the end ones. It's not as loud as if you would kick it, but it's enough to make a difference, and if you put a mic to

differently, and depending on which one you accent through the PA, you get a different sound. Sometimes you want a little more live sound, so you just mess with the faders and you can balance it out front.

I use 12", 13", 14", 18", and 20" toms, and then I use three of the latest Simmons and two Rototoms. I used to have five rack toms, but it just got to the point where I didn't need to have little concert toms. If it's not necessary, I don't use it. It's not just for trying to create the biggest drumset in the world. I had the concert toms, but it made it very difficult for me to see Ed onstage, who I really mainly play off of, and secondly, I can get that kind of sound just by tuning the 12" up a little higher, and then anything else can be played with the Simmons.

MD: Your rack toms are single headed?
Alex: Yeah. Especially live, where you don't really have a great ambience. Sometimes we use double heads in the studio, because the studio is a little more adaptable to that situation. The bleed from the other instruments is

"I think that a lot of people take it

I've seen a lot of people where, when they get offstage, they're completely different people. There's no genuine feel behind it. That's why the timeless performers are the same offstage as they are on, and it shows. Some people put on a funny suit or funny clothes and think, "Hey, I'm going to get a haircut just like this guy, get the guitar that looks like this guy, play like this guy, move like somebody else… how come nothing is happening?" The feel just isn't there. Maybe one album, maybe two, but I think longevity is if you're really into it. We've been together for ten years, even though we've only been recording for five or six.

MD: Let's talk about your elaborate equipment.
Alex: Okay. First, God created the bass drum.
MD: And Alex uses six?
Alex: Well, it is six because the two main ones I play are joined together. They're actually 28" long, which started because the projection is much better. For some reason, I got a much better punch onstage when I had a

it, it gets a little bit more resonance. There's no dampening of any kind except for a felt strip on the inside ones, and that's it.
MD: When did you start using the kicks joined together?
Alex: That was after the first album was recorded, during the hiatus between the recording time and the time we went on tour. That was when we had the time to test stuff out onstage and found that the longer bass drum had more projection in a specific direction. Shortly thereafter, Ludwig came out with their longer bass drum.
MD: How are the middle drums connected?
Alex: Just bolted together, air-tight. Billy Cobham was the first one who started screwing around with this by using two snares and three bass drums, and everybody said, "Wait a minute—how does he play three bass drums?" It works for me and makes sense. It may not be everybody's cup of tea, but for me it works. I like it because it gives me a wider range of acoustics. Each drum is tuned

not there, so you can tape a little bit further from the drums, such as having an overhead that will do only drums and pick up room ambience. Since we don't really have to worry about re-patching guitar and playing it again because some of it does leak onto the drum track, there's no problem. We play that song straight through and it's there. If you start doctoring it and say, "Wait a minute, this guitar part needs to get out and put something else in, then you're in trouble, but we don't need that.
MD: What about miking for a live situation?
Alex: How I keep the monitor I use from bleeding into the different drums is I use a limiter, which is set at the frequency of the drums so it picks up only that drum and nothing else. I'm sure a lot of people have the problem when a guitarist plays, you really have a hard time hearing what's going on. So I have a special setup, which is a cabinet that's a direct hook-up to Ed's amp, so it doesn't even go through a monitor system. It's an identical cabinet he plays through. For the drum

mix, that goes through a side monitor guy, who sits there and has the sixteen channels. During the soundcheck, that will be adjusted and then we adjust the noise gates to the point where nothing bleeds through.

When you're playing at such a high volume, problems you encounter tend to multiply, but after all the trials and the testing, we finally found how things work best for us. I'm sure our sound man would say, "Wait a minute—you guys really can play quieter onstage. Come on, have a little control." But there's a certain point where you draw the line, and that's how we wanted it.

MD: Of course the question that comes up is do you really need all that wattage?

Alex: It depends on where you play. You obviously don't want to make it uncomfortably loud for everybody, but at the same time, you want it to project across the whole thing. You have to feel the music as well as hear it, and it's one big package. That's one

somebody who has a good ear, because the sound mixer out front is your producer on the road. You can be playing the best stuff you ever played in your life, but if the sound isn't good, what's the point? And that includes anything from the balance of the instruments, to the tonality, to the way the speakers are set up, to the hall itself.

In one respect soundcheck is almost pointless, because the sound changes so drastically by the time people get in. But it gives you a good point to start at and especially to make sure everything works. It's a tedious thing, but we always do it. I just wouldn't get up there if I didn't know what it sounded like. We usually will tape a piece and then play it back and stand out front to see how it sounds. You can't really go by one person's ear. Everybody has different tastes, and what might sound good to one person might not be what somebody else likes. We also have reference tapes we listen to.

MD: How do you protect your ears?

It's something that most drummers I'm sure can identify with, especially in loud situations where the ride cymbal just really chews into your ear. At the end of the night, it's called noise drunk. You don't hear any more highs, and you kind of feel alienated when you're finished playing. It happens. I guess if you can get used to earplugs, it might be a good idea. But it's just one of those things that comes with the territory.

MD: Tuning. Is there a method to your madness?

Alex: Each drum has an inherent quality. You don't tune it to a note, really. The best thing is to make the individual drum sound the best it can to itself. You can't make a floor tom sound like a little concert tom. You just play with it until it sounds like the drum. Certain drums have certain frequencies that respond well. You can tell when you're out of it—below it or above it—and when you hit that right spot, there it is.

MD: You mentioned before that you

too seriously when they get up onstage. They're out to change the course of history."

of the things that used to impress me when I was younger and I would go see Black Sabbath. You could feel that kick drum go right through your chest. I said, "I want to do that!"

We carry the most extensive sound system that anybody ever takes on the road. We don't sell our audiences short by cutting back on sound. I think we usually carry about 40,000 watts, which is twice what most bands use, but the difference is the same thing as if you were to take a transistor radio and turn it full blast and get the distortion, or take a nice stereo and play it halfway. Sure, you encounter certain problems, but the one thing we always do demand is that we get an extensive soundcheck and we have all the best sound men available. For our kind of setup, it works.

It took us four years to really get the best situation happening with

Alex: [laughs] I don't. Over the last fifteen years, I've lost twenty percent in my left ear and fifteen percent in my right ear. It just comes with the job. If you want to be able to hear what's going on, you can't really effectively use any kind of earplug. I was thinking of using cotton because it does help to cut the super highs out. When I went to the doctor, he gave me a dB meter to go out and actually measure what was happening. The chart he gave me said that if you're exposed to about 110 decibels, you can get away with it for about half an hour before there are any dangerous side effects. He told me that with 120, you can last for about five minutes. So we went to a rehearsal, and before the monitors were on and before any of the sound was plugged in, with just straight drums, I was banging away at the cymbals a little bit, and it was already 130.

like a live snare sound. How do you achieve that?

Alex: I like to have mine tuned a little higher than the average person. The best person I can use as an example is Bonham. His snare is tuned pretty high. I'm not saying high to the point where it sounds like a concert snare with a little pop, but not like a thud, although we've done that. In the studio, you do a variety of things, but I prefer that higher sound. The best way I can describe it is almost like chopping wood. It has the attack and the resonance, but it also has a lot of sound to it and a lot of mid. Everybody has his own taste, though.

Original interview by Robyn Flans.

• YAMAHA MAPLE CUSTOMS • NIRVANA'S DAVE GROHL

MODERN
DRUMMER®
The World's Most Widely Read Drum Magazine
JULY '93

ALEX
VAN HALEN

SINATRA'S
GREGG FIELD

'93 READERS
POLL RESULTS

PLUS:
• A LOOK AT FALICON
• IN THE STUDIO WITH MICHAEL BLAIR
• EDDIE BAYERS ON COUNTRY DRUMMING

Live at Last
The 1993 Interview

Modern Drummer's second AVH cover story came on the occasion of their first live album/DVD, *Right Here, Right Now*, which hit a full fifteen years after Van Halen exploded onto the scene with their iconic debut album. It had also been ten years since Alex's last *MD* cover, a period that saw the replacement of singer David Lee Roth with rock vet Sammy Hagar, as well as the construction of their own studio, 5150. It was there that we spent an enlightening afternoon with Alex, who happily showed us around, screened some of the brand-new VH live footage, and answered our questions for a solid two hours.

MD: Since this new album is live, let's talk a little about the concert situation.

Alex: We feel a special bond with the audience. A lot of people just seem to think of it in terms of, "Well, let's fill this building and make a lot of money." But I am as much a fan of the music as I am a player. Omar Hakim told a story once about a gig he played along with a lot of big drummers, and some of them were really concerned about outplaying the other guys. But Omar just had this real friendly vibe and said, "Hey man, I'm going to the gig as a fan, too. I'm just gonna enjoy it, and whatever happens happens." That says it all. You take it as it comes—which is basically how we did this live record.

MD: The album includes material from the past few tours. How did you choose which songs were included?

Alex: We picked whatever we felt kicked our butt. But we didn't look for perfection. We just wanted the vibe. If we went into the studio and fixed things, it wouldn't be a live record anymore. If you start patching and pasting, what's the point? And see, we couldn't do it because there were these video cameras. [laughs]

MD: So you didn't have to deal with that sticky ethical stuff.

Alex: Yeah, right. But really, what would be the point? This was a step out for us as much as it was for the audience.

MD: How come so long for a live album? You guys have been recording for fifteen years.

Alex: Well, in '86, when Sammy joined the band, we didn't feel that doing a lot of material prior to that would have been an accurate representation of the band. The reason we never had a live record out before '86 was because the vocals just weren't there. Not to be judgmental, but it just wasn't happening. So we waited until we felt the time was right. Besides, we wanted to get the studio stuff out first. When we're inspired and think the music we come up with is worth listening to, we want to get it out. If you put out a live record, it's going to get in the way, scheduling-wise, of whatever studio stuff you do. But now we felt that the material was there, and everything just fell into place.

MD: How do you keep motivated after touring for so long? Even before the band got signed you were playing out a lot.

Alex: It was actually tougher then, because that was five

"Live playing is just the embodiment of what we're all about."

hours a night—and it wasn't even our own material.

MD: So how do you stay so into it for so long? Is it purely the energy off the audience?

Alex: It's a combination of things. I think you're born a musician. It's not something you pick up because you saw it on MTV. It's in your blood. Buddy Rich played until the day he died, more or less. I know a lot of guys who play out maybe once a month, hoping that the record companies will come that particular night and give them a deal. Musicians make music and they go out and play. If you can't handle traveling around the world and living out of a suitcase, then maybe it's not the right thing.

MD: How about early on, when you were doing five-hour nights?

Alex: I think everybody has a dream, and dreams can be more powerful than anything. It gives you something to aim and focus at, and it makes everything else—the pain, if there is any—it just makes that go away. Playing gives you so much joy, you know, you almost feel guilty. "How come I like what I'm doing so much?"

MD: How has the live thing changed over the years?

Alex: There are so many things going on live as far as what assaults your senses. There's not only the playing, but the audience is going nuts. For good or bad we are one of the loudest bands—onstage anyway. Out front we are legally limited to 110 or 120 dBs, so we're very careful with that. As far as equipment, a monitor is a monitor—until you get a guy who tweaks the wrong frequencies and your ears go, which does happen. We've been fortunate, though, on the last tour in particular. We had some great guys.

MD: How about headphones? You wear them on a couple of songs to hear a sequencer. Does that present any special problems?

Alex: As far as this whole concept of having sequenced music: Edward only has five arms, and some of the recorded stuff has keyboards and guitar. Sammy thinks that, to maintain the integrity of the song, it's better if Ed plays it. So every three days or so, Ed plays the keyboard parts during soundcheck while I'm playing, and it goes into a sequencer. But it has all the inconsistencies of him playing; it's not like a track from the record. So it may speed up and slow down or whatever. All I've got to do is hopefully be in the same frame of mind and listen to the inconsistencies. The only thing that bothered me in the beginning was the possibility that, God forbid, the headphones blow up, or something whacky happens—then I can't hear anything. And then we're all up the creek without a paddle. If I'm playing with Ed while he's playing and something goes askew, hey, we'll improvise.

MD: Not only is the new album live, but you've also released a live video.

Alex: I think the video is probably the most accurate representation of the band. Live playing is just the embodiment of what we're all

about. And we take the playing aspect of it very seriously. If somebody isn't playing up to par, they're going to hear about it. On the other side of the coin, the kind of music we make is not exactly quantum theory.

MD: Sometimes that makes mistakes more obvious.

Alex: It sure does. I'm glad you mentioned that, because people say, "Yeah, this guy just does 2/4 shit. What is this crap?" I remember in one issue of *Modern Drummer*, Mickey Curry was talking about his involvement with certain songs, and that sometimes the simpler it seemed, the more complex and difficult it really was, because things stick out much more than when there's a lot of shit going on.

See, I never really sat down in the beginning with a metronome and did your traditional practicing. What we did was we played, and you learn as much, if not more, by playing with other musicians. Because in music there are just so many more things than just being able to play your instrument.

MD: The old jazz guys say things like, "We never had to practice because we were always out playing...."

Alex: That's right. I actually started out playing jazz. I was thirteen years old on my first paying gig. One of the things I was most impressed by was playing with these guys in their forties. It wasn't a casual, it was a step above that. These guys made records, and I just happened to luck into this kind of thing because the drummer couldn't make it at the last minute. But music tore down all the barriers as far as age or background. Once you were on this playing field, everybody was an equal—as long as you played well. For me it was very insightful in terms of how music is such an interactive thing—not only among the musicians, but among the audience as well. You learn to improvise. It's like, "Keep that train rolling on the track." I

mean, the little missed cues, hey, I'm thirteen. [laughs]

MD: What specific things might a rock drummer learn from listening to jazz?

Alex: I think the biggest mistake any drummer can make is to listen to one kind of music. Rhythm is the foundation of everything. When somebody listens to a tune on the radio, the first thing they do is either tap their foot or snap their fingers. Drumming has been around for as long as people can remember—for communication, for leading armies into battle. It's the most instinctive instrument; people instinctively feel the rhythm.

When you listen to different types of music, it's more important to capture the *spirit* of what you're listening to than what somebody's doing note-for-note. You've got to feel it on a bigger scale. You learn to listen to how the musicians interact. I've always looked at playing your instrument as a different way of talking or communicating. If one player is doing something, don't mimic him note-for-note, but kind of get the *feeling* of what he's doing. Of course, you're limited by how well you can play, but that's why you practice, so you get to the point where, when the thought comes into your head, you can execute it.

It's like learning a language. You learn word by word until eventually you don't have to think about how you patch it together. I'm not saying learn lick-by-lick, but do your rudiments at least. I didn't practice rudiments until about the second record. All the things I learned were things I had heard before, and I played my interpretation of what I heard.

MD: Taking the rudiments/language thing a bit further, there are certain writers where you can kind of tell they're trying to use the language very consciously.

Alex: Oh yeah, because they use these regular sixth-grade mentality words, and all of a sudden a word pops up that you've got to look up in the dictionary.

MD: Well, then is playing drums kind of the same thing? Because you've got to take this language—rudiments—

and you have to apply them but not *sound* like you are.

Alex: The drums have different colors, different textures, and you can do lots of things—within limits by the fact that you only have four limbs, and within the limits of the song. Once in a while you hear these ballads on the radio. They're cruising along with a nice feel, and all of a sudden, [Alex mimics a wild drum fill]. What was

of using tonality, all you ever hear is, [Alex mimics a simple descending tom fill]. Okay, fine. But I think it was Buddy Rich who said, "The less you use, the more creative you become," because you're painted into a corner, so to speak. And you have to use a little bit more ingenuity or creativity. It was actually Leonardo da Vinci who said, "Large rooms distract the mind; small rooms focus the mind." If you have too

cymbal. But of course at some point you've got to play them, because everybody's going to be looking. So yeah, you go over there and play them for no reason at all. [laughs]

MD: Well, what about just physically reaching some of this stuff? You've had some pretty big setups. Was it ever a problem actually hitting things?

Alex: No, I reached it all. I think it was in 1988 that I had a kit that was three

that? Okay, so you learned this new thing. So it's like what you were saying about sticking something in out of the blue—it's a little inconsistent. I think maybe that comes from time and experience. And the best way to get that is by playing with other people.

MD: You just mentioned limitations. It's been said that limitations can be good—like if you've only got a certain number of notes to play, those notes will mean more.

Alex: Absolutely. As a matter of fact, last year I went to a smaller drumkit. A couple of toms, kick drum, a snare, and a couple cymbals. And yeah, when you've got ten toms, instead

much to pick from, you get confused. If your focus is narrowed down, it gives you much more of a sense of direction on what you can do.

MD: So was shrinking your kit down a conscious decision?

Alex: I think instinctively you go through phases; you kind of feel like it's time for a change. And at the time that's what I felt.

MD: As drummers, it seems we tend to add things to our kits and then figure out what to do with them later.

Alex: Oh, yeah. I remember in 1980, I had these Rototoms that were really just so damn far to reach, but they looked nice up there, tucked under a

drumsets put together. I only played one of them at a time, but they were all different. One was a North drumset, one was an electronic kit, and one was an acoustic drumset, and it was all on a rotating stage. And for whatever song that I needed a particular sound, I would just rotate the stage. It was that simple. But there were visual considerations. I don't mean, "Yeah, let's put on the make-up and make our hair stand on end." But there is something to be said about the visual aspect of drumming. Some of it is natural just because you're in motion. Right there it's already a physical or visual thing.

We were playing on a stage that was a hundred twenty-five feet wide. That's roughly three times as wide as your average arena stage, and to have this small drumset in the middle of it looked very strange. I wasn't about to put up a hundred drums and not use any of them, so that was part of the reason for this setup. It all worked out, and I was very happy with that.

MD: You're using permanently mounted mics inside your drums. Does that work out pretty good for you?

Alex: It works out ten thousand times better than anything else I've ever done. That's because the mic is isolated. You have much more control over the gain. If a mic is out in the open, you have to put limiters or noise gates on, which means the lighter notes aren't going to be heard. And everything else bleeds into it, so there's less control. Then add to that the fact that we're loud onstage—which we have to be because the audience is loud. We need to hear what we're playing. We call it the gas wars. You know, one thing comes up, and before you know it everyone is running at peak volume and the speakers can't take it anymore—not to mention your ears.

MD: It's the same thing for bands on small stages, isn't it?

Alex: Oh, yeah. When we played the clubs, the cymbals alone were enough to deafen everybody.

MD: Going through the mics?

Alex: No, just if somebody was standing near a cymbal at ear level going SHHHHH! Everybody would back away from the drums—which was actually fine with me. [laughs]

MD: You mentioned before about the really large stages. When you got to the point where you were all of a sudden playing large stages, were there any new playing considerations because of that?

Alex: I think in the beginning—and

YAMAHA MAPLE CUSTOMS • NIRVANA'S DAVE GROHL

MODERN DRUMMER

The World's Most Widely Read Drum Magazine

JULY '93

ALEX VAN HALEN

SINATRA'S GREGG FIELD

'93 READERS POLL RESULTS

PLUS:
• A LOOK AT FALICON
• IN THE STUDIO WITH MICHAEL BLAIR
• EDDIE BAYERS ON COUNTRY DRUMMING

this didn't really last long—but when you're playing on a large stage and there are thousands of people, the first tendency is to just over-hammer the shit, because you think it's not going to come out. Playing through microphones and PA systems was new to me, and it took maybe a month or two to get out of the habit of wanting to just drown everything, because it doesn't make any difference. At a certain point a drum just does not get any louder.

MD: You can also start cramping up when you don't realize how hard you're playing, right?

Alex: Yeah, but I think you also have to remember that there is a sense of excitement. I think the moment a

> "The drummer is the most powerful guy in the band, because he can speed things up, he can slow things down—he can stop the whole damn thing."

player becomes blasé about walking onstage—that's the time to hang it up. There should always be a feeling of excitement, but you have to channel that energy. You don't want to walk out in front of 20,000 people and just go "WAAAAA!" even though you feel like it. I'll be honest with you, that is

how you feel. But if you can just stay loose, it's fine. We're at it two and a half hours, and we're hammering. We don't hold back. But you don't blow everything all at once, either. You can have that excitement in your heart and in your mind, but your body stays loose. And after about two songs or so, you're really into a groove and you're just transported into a different place. I can't describe it. I guess athletes call it an endorphin rush or something. At the end of the night, there's a great "Ahhhh," a release. It's very satisfying.

MD: Are there some specific things that one can do to loosen up?

Alex: I think the best thing is to just concentrate and tell yourself, "Stay loose." And after a while it becomes natural.

MD: How about physically staying loose before a show? What do you do?

Alex: It takes me about a half hour to warm up. You know, you don't go running twenty-five miles without stretching a little bit.

MD: Do you do rudiments on the pad?

Alex: Yeah…you see, all those things I take for granted. That just comes with the territory. It's something that…who wants to know how many hours somebody practices? If you're into something, it should be totally consuming. The drums for me are probably the most all-encompassing instrument, because it takes your brains, it takes your heart, it takes a commitment—it obviously takes your physical ability. Let's face it, you have to be able to do certain things or you can't pull it off.

MD: Let's change gears for a minute. A lot of younger drummers seem to have trouble orchestrating parts to a song—changing their parts during the chorus, verse, bridge, or whatever. You've always done that in interesting ways.

Alex: I look at it like counterbalancing what's going on with the guitar. I guess some people describe it as finding the hole and filling it. It's not quite that simple—at least not on every song. Some songs are just downright straightforward. There's no way but to play 2/4 and do whatever you feel is right. Other songs, like "Spank," are wide open. I hear brass

punches here and there and I'll accent them.

The good thing about music, and what drums have done for me, is that it puts your ego aside. You have to listen. You learn more from listening than from telling other people how smart you are. If somebody makes a

suggestion about what you're playing, don't let your ego get instantly deflated. The whole idea is working towards a common thing.

I don't think I've ever mentioned it before, but I've played guitar, I've played saxophone, I played violin for four or five years, I've played piano for sixteen years, and believe it or not I have a degree in scoring and arranging. As far as "traditional" music training, the people in this band have had a lot. Whether it manifests itself in our music, who knows? I think the moment you become too technical, you lose all the heart and the feeling of it. But you can't help but have some of what you learned filter in and make you more knowledgeable about what you're doing. Some things, like song structure, are very obvious to me. In rock 'n' roll, you're dealing with a format that's three to four minutes long, and you have to make that piece of music make sense to the listener.

That in and of itself is an art form.

I would say that, if you're at all inclined, play different instruments so you have a sense of what they do. The more you know about everything, the better it is. You can have a real sense of what's going on.

I also think that, even though I

played all those instruments, with none of them did I feel the connection I did with drums. Now, some people might say, "Well, of course, because the drums are the easiest instrument to play." Well, I say, "You try it for a while." But everybody has a gift. Like Ed, for instance—I could practice until doomsday and I would never be able to play the way he does. And there's no connection between me and the strings. With drums there is.

MD: One drummer you've mentioned in the past as inspirational is Ringo.

Alex: One of the most interesting things about Ringo is how he managed to maintain a level of self-esteem—in addition to being a great player, of course. But he wasn't overshadowed as a human being by McCartney or Lennon or Harrison. I think he did a wonderful thing for drums because drummers would see him and think, "Hey, he's part of it too."

MD: Maybe drummers were told that they were separate from the rest of the band for so long that we began to believe it ourselves.

Alex: Well, yeah, maybe, but I think some of that is brought on by us, too. If you don't know much about what you're doing other than the beat…. Whether you want to admit it or not, there is a certain hierarchy, so to speak, in music. "I'm the lead guitarist! He's the rhythm guitarist." Now what does that tell you? "Oh, and by the way, he's the drummer. What's your name again?" You know? It's just the nature of the instruments. People tend to think that for some reason the lead singer or front man is more intelligent. Drummers, by the nature of the instrument, are put slightly behind the scenes. But it's actually a great place because not only are you providing the foundation, but the drive, the push. The drummer is actually the most powerful guy in the band because he can speed things up, he can slow things down—he can stop the whole damn thing. The guitarist can stop, but if the drummer keeps playing, people still think the song's going.

MD: Let's talk about your drum sound. It's always been unique and identifiable.

Alex: Ever since I can remember, it wasn't only somebody's playing style that really impressed me, it was also their sound. Ginger Baker's drums sounded like Ginger Baker's drums. Bonham sounded like Bonham, even though there was a change from the third record to the fourth. Your instrument is like your second voice. It's the way you communicate. I think the way that an instrument sounds is as important as what you're playing on it. I've spent a

YAMAHA MAPLE CUSTOMS • NIRVANA'S DAVE GROHL

MODERN DRUMMER

The World's Most Widely Read Drum Magazine

JULY '93

ALEX VAN HALEN

SINATRA'S GREGG FIELD

'93 READERS POLL RESULTS

PLUS:
• A LOOK AT FALICON
• IN THE STUDIO WITH MICHAEL BLAIR
• EDDIE BAYERS ON COUNTRY DRUMMING

U.S. $3.95
U.K. £2.00
Canada $4.95

attitude toward their sound?

Alex: The first thing is you've got to be flexible. I can use our first record as an example. Having never made a record or been in a bona fide studio, I had all these dreams: "Wow, this is going to be amazing! The drums are going to sound like I never heard before." I get there and the first thing [producer] Ted Templeman says is, "Take that front head off the kick drum and the bottom heads off the toms." My jaw

unique and interesting it was and how much he loved it. So I shut my mouth, [laughs] and I thought, this shows me something: Once it's on record, and somebody else has heard it, their interpretation is as important as what you thought you wanted. There's this old Zen saying: There are no inherently good or bad things; it's just your interpretation. So something I was initially extremely dissatisfied with turned out for the better.

MD: Van Halen records have usually had a very live vibe, right from the first album. At that time, things were really structured in the studios. But it seems like you were given some playing freedom.

Alex: If there were any limitations,

"Your instrument is like your second

lot of time with the guys for the live shows to get it how I like it, and it's difficult because on record it's not always been recorded the way I like it. On the earlier records the drums were the last thing that anybody ever checked for sound. It's something I wasn't happy with, but it's something you deal with.

MD: Do you have an optimum sound in your head as a point of reference?

Alex: Yeah, but I haven't gotten it yet. [laughs] It gives you something to go for, though.

MD: Where have you gotten the closest to that sound?

Alex: On this live record, I think the snare drum is damn close. Again, in a live situation you're obviously not as controlled as in the studio. But there are little bits and pieces where I'm very happy. The nature of certain songs also affects the sound. The faster the song, the more careful you've got to be with the delays. The size of the room you're in and how the drums are tuned also affect the sound. Drums are much more important to the overall sound than a lot of people—guitarists, whoever—will admit.

MD: Well, following that point, what would you suggest to drummers having a rough time dealing with another musician's or producer's

dropped. I was ready to explode, but it was not my place to do that. I knew enough about myself to say, "Just leave the room, calm down, then come back in." And when I came back in, sure enough, the drumheads had been pulled.

Be flexible. Your time will come. If you're really a musician, you have your whole life in front of you to get your sound. And I think that part of the fun is that whatever it is you're reaching for, it's always just a little bit out of reach. That not only provides the motivation, but it keeps the dream alive. If everything was perfect, then what would you do?

MD: Back to the first album….

Alex: I don't mean to say it wasn't fun. It was an honor and a pleasure to work with somebody like Ted Templeman, because he was very well respected, and rightly so. He really knew how to put things together. But the drum sound was not what I wanted. Now, of course, the problem is that everybody has heard that album, and they say, "Oh, I love that drum sound!" and I say, "Well, it is what it is."

I had the opportunity to meet Jim Keltner and Ringo, and Jim started to talk about the record *5150*. I was just about to tell him what I didn't like about it, and he told me how

they were brought on by ourselves, because of the fact that it was our first record. The idea of three people playing together beginning to end was unusual at that point. But Ted wanted the uniqueness of the band playing as an ensemble, and that's what was great about it. And of course you don't take as many chances because, God forbid, you're the one who messed up the take: "Now we've got to do it all over again."

MD: It still came across sounding more live than your average album from the time.

Alex: Oh yeah, absolutely. But had it been up to us, man, it would've been Cream revisited. [laughs]

MD: How about now that you've got this studio? Does that change things?

Alex: I hate to say that we're "smart" enough now, but we can instinctively tell when something becomes stagnant. You could record the perfect record, at least in terms of getting on record everything you wanted to do. But then the spontaneity and uniqueness of playing together is lost.

We'll use a hypothetical day. For the last record, the songs were more or less written one at a time and recorded as they were written. So it's been a week, we've worked on the song, we're happy with the sounds, Andy has adjusted the microphones.

At the end of the day, we'll run it down one more time and see what we think of it. The next day, the first thing, we just mentally gear ourselves up the same way we would for a gig, and just put everything into it. We'll play a song two times—that's it. If we didn't get it that day, we leave it. We'll spend the rest of the day working on something else. Either it's there or it ain't. And we're the ones who know. There were little things on the last record where technically they could have been a little bit better, but it would have lost the feel.

MD: If you listen to old Kinks or Who records, there were times when that stuff was a little sloppy, but it's not like people were thinking about that me before that a big part of it for you is getting something back from the audience.

Alex: When you play for people you get instant response. I think if you were alone in a room and you were going to record a drum solo, you would play different things. Live, you don't know what's going to happen with the audience, which is the fun part about it. There will be a kind of swell in the audience, and they'll pick up on certain things—which may not necessarily be the most technical things you do.

Musically, a solo is a different texture altogether. I look at it like I'm playing a song, it's just that nobody else is playing along with me. It gives whole night my mind would only be focused on the solo, which is kind of a strange way to think. But then again, you're the only one playing at the time, so if something goes wrong, it's much more obvious. You can't hide behind the bass player. But part of the beauty of a solo is, since there *is* no one else playing, it's the most improvisational time. It's not necessarily just a self-indulgent ego trip. I don't look at it that way because, quite honestly, just from a physical standpoint, it would be a cakewalk to play two and a half hours without doing that.

MD: You told me earlier that you haven't actually played for a week or so. Does it feel different after you've

voice. It's the way you communicate. I think the way that an instrument sounds is as important as what you're playing on it."

when they first heard it.

Alex: Hey, Keith Moon was a big influence on me. I just thought that he was the *embodiment* of drummers. He was the guy who was over the edge, going a hundred ninety-five miles an hour all the time. But you know, you kind of take a little bit from this and a little bit from that and put it all together.

MD: You've put a version of "Won't Get Fooled Again" on the live album.

Alex: Yeah, in the middle of a gig we always pick out something to play, and that night it happened to be "Won't Get Fooled Again." It's kind of weird, because you listen to what Moon did, and you don't want to do it note-for-note. But at the same time you've got to cop his kind of feel, because that was a major part of their music. So it's always an iffy thing, and let's face it, the Who, Zeppelin—you don't redo that stuff to make it better. You can't.

MD: Let's talk about soloing. You told me more latitude to do what I want and also be back and forth with the audience. As far as a drum solo being a "showcase" for things that you couldn't do in songs, though…well, you've got a problem if you need to show what you can play in a solo. That just means you're not really applying everything you know in the songs.

MD: How structured are your solos?

Alex: It's not thought out note-for-note, but on the live album, for instance, it's in three pieces. There is a theme, which is a five count and a seven count. Then I'll put something underneath, like the kick drum, that's static. That way, when you put something else against it, you'll know that it's changing.

The first part is an odd meter, seven against four and five against four; the middle part is in 4/4, even though I'm flopping around a little bit; and the last part is the same as the first, only it's against three now instead of four. You know, I found early on that the taken a break and then play again?

Alex: That's a good point. Sometimes you step away from it and you come back and it's invigorating. It's like, "Hey, wow! I didn't notice I had it down that good." It gives you an edge. You've got to be careful. You have to listen to yourself, your body, your rhythm. If you're touring too long, and it's really becoming work, and there isn't that edge, it's unfair to the audience.

Being a musician, you're covering one extreme to the other. On the one hand, it is the most selfish thing, because you're making music and you want to play it exactly the way you want. On the other hand, you've got to think about the audience—particularly when you're playing live. They came to see you at your best. You owe it to them to give them your all.

Original interview by Adam Budofsky

Bashing and Crashing in the Here and Now
The 2008 Interview

On their 2007–2008 tour, Van Halen reunited with original singer David Lee Roth for the first time since he'd left the band in 1985. It wasn't the only major lineup change: Eddie's son Wolfgang took over bass duties from Michael Anthony, doubling the buzz surrounding the shows, and helping make it the band's most profitable run to date. *Modern Drummer* caught up with Alex following their show at New Jersey's Meadowlands arena.

MD: It's been a long while since the last Van Halen tour. What did you do to get back in road shape?

Alex: Ed and I play every day. So I didn't have to get back in shape. Ed has the 5150 Studios on his property in Studio City; we have a routine. It's the one forced discipline that we have. We play once a day, every day. We play for a couple of hours, sometimes less, sometimes more. Sometimes things evolve. Ed has ideas, and often something I'm playing will trigger an idea. But there's no goal in mind. It's not,

"Let's pretend to be creative and make a record."

MD: What's your setup at the studio? How many bass drums?

Alex: The only reason I use two bass drums at all is because my right foot just isn't fast enough for some of the stuff

I like to do, especially some of the shuffles. When it comes down to what you really need when you're playing, you use your hi-hat, snare, ride, and kick drum. Honestly, I think the more gear you have, the less creative you'll be.

Normally in the studio I use a snare, a kick, a hi-hat, and a cymbal—and maybe one tom. When you're trying to be creative, I've found that a smaller setup—and varying it up—helps. Otherwise you fall into the same old patterns. And you can be distracted by too much stuff.

MD: Your technique is very supple and flexible, and your wrists are so loose. At the Meadowlands gig you played like you had rubber bands for arms. Also, your sticking is very high off the drums. Is that the result of staying loose? What else figures into your approach?

Alex: It's in part because I've had problems with tendinitis. To be supple when you play, you have to be relaxed. I do Shudokan martial arts just to stay relaxed while I'm exerting myself. Every little bit of tension creates a problem. It's such a cliché: They tell you to relax. But actually doing it is tricky. You have to be relaxed.

MD: What got you into martial arts?

Alex: It stems from an injury; I fractured my neck twenty years ago. Ten years ago, it became a problem. In fact, I was walking around with a neck brace. I had to keep that damn thing around my neck. It kept my neck in alignment. If it got out of alignment, my arm and leg would go numb. My neck was being strangled by the disc tissue.

MD: I imagine the doctors said you shouldn't be playing the drums.

Alex: Of course! [laughs] It started in '95, when I was at Wolfgang's birthday party at Disney World. I collapsed for no apparent reason. Long story short, it went back to my herniating four discs and fracturing all the bones in my neck. It was caused by a water skiing accident. After the accident, I was paralyzed for an hour, then everything came back, no problem. Then ten years later, because my body compensated for so long, it just locked up.

MD: Didn't you ever feel any prickly

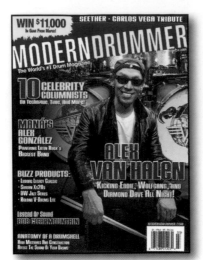

pains?

Alex: Oh, yeah. I just ignored it. But when I collapsed, it was the beginning of our Balance tour, and that wasn't fun. So I began studying martial arts, working on posture and the Alexander technique, which shows you how to use your body correctly.

My favorite position for drumming was always a cigarette in one hand and a drink in the other. [Alex mimics a hunched-over posture and traditional grip.] And checking out the women. [laughs]

MD: You initially played traditional grip.

Alex: Oh, yeah, but the guitar and bass were so loud I had to change to matched. Ed and I began by playing jazz; our dad would take us to clubs and we would sit in with jazz groups. I can't explain it other than to say those early experiences are very deeply rooted in my DNA. I understand the relationship between music and an audience and how it works in the dynamic of an evening.

MD: You can hear the jazz influence in your playing, because once again, it's loose yet propulsive at the same time. Your looseness surprised me; your drumming was supple and effortless, which we don't always equate with hard rock or proto-metal drumming.

Alex: It didn't always sound like that. You go through changes. The '80s were different from the '90s. When Ginger Baker was asked what the drummer's role was in a band, he said it was "to make the other musicians sound good." He didn't mean it as an arrogant statement, but I now know what he meant. You want to fit in with the music. You could be a Buddy Rich, but you can't do all those things when you're playing a simple song. You have to play what's appropriate for the tune. Jeff Porcaro understood that. He knew how to make things move without sticking out as though he was trying to solo.

In the '80s, our music was a little more bombastic. We tried to position ourselves as being unique and to show our best qualities. All those different elements led me to crash and bash.

MD: If you were bashing and crashing in

the '80s, how would you compare that style to what you're doing now?

Alex: Oh…refined. Back then we didn't want anyone to know that we had gone through classical training and that our main instrument was the piano. Jazz was what we really started with, and that's a lot different from rock 'n' roll.

I read an interesting article with Steve Smith where he talked about the difference between straight time and the idea of a pulse. That was something I always understood but couldn't articulate. The point is that my brother and I began as a two-piece, and the whole idea is that you want to groove together. When we were putting a song together, because we had a classical background, we knew that you use dynamics and rhythm changes to your advantage. The idea of trying to create strict metronomic time is nonsense. When you come to a part that needs a moment, you take a breath and slow down. Then you ramp it up and bring the volume up.

When I listen to our early records, the time fluctuates, because the music breathes. Instead of having it in a box, it's an organic thing. Most of it you don't even notice because you're caught up in the music.

MD: But Van Halen probably used a click on its last few albums.

Alex: I learned how to do that. Instead of playing to a click, you think of it as playing along with another guy in the band. You can play "around" it.

MD: Do you follow a practice regimen, and does that lead into your pre-gig warm-up?

Alex: Before the show I just kind of zone out and "ticky tack." I play through the rudiments. One show I was sitting backstage with the drummer for Kenny Chesney, and he showed me an exercise I'd never seen before. You play a shuffle with your left hand, the quarter note and two dotted 8ths on your right hand, and then add triplets with the right foot, but only the last two strokes of the triplet. You can play the first note of the triplet with your hi-hat. That's a blast.

MD: Is that one way you keep it interesting for yourself?

Alex: Being in a band is more than just music. From the very beginning it had a lot to do with the Beatles and how good they were at their publicity machine. I thought *A Hard Day's Night* was for real. The impact that music can have on the fabric of how people perceive things as being popular, how that resonates on a larger level—that's something that always fascinated me. How can this band be something bigger than just the four of us? That takes a certain give and take. It's not about me and my space, it's about us.

MD: Are you saying that you're more concerned about the band overall than working on your technique?

Alex: Yes.

MD: But as a drummer, you have to keep your chops up.

Alex: I know that. [laughs] It's ninety percent practice and the other ten percent is…talent.

MD: So playing the drums is just second-nature to you, like putting on a pair of jeans?

Alex: Well, Ed and I both played piano, but I gravitated to the drums. When my dad's band would practice at the house, I would jump on the drums. They felt very natural to me. If the drummer couldn't make it to my dad's gig, I would fill in.

MD: So how long do you warm up now before a show?

Alex: Thirty minutes. I usually play on a pillow. I don't like a pad. I like something with no rebound.

I had the pleasure of meeting and taking a lesson with Jim Chapin. He sat down at the kit and showed me a few things, but I really just wanted to vibe off of him. He's eighty years old, but still excited and interested—he's alive. When he completed the lesson, I said, "Thank you very much." And he said, "That'll be eighty dollars." [laughs] I paid him and gave him a ride.

MD: What did Chapin focus on in the lesson?

Alex: Just Moeller technique. I probably didn't study Moeller as much as I should have, but I do it.

MD: Does Moeller figure into your very high sticking?

Alex: A little bit. And working on tension-and-release. I've been doing this for forty years, so you want to make sure nothing breaks. I play more German than French grip.

MD: Are you still actively trying to push your drumming forward?

Alex: Well, I'll let Vinnie [Colaiuta] do that. [laughs] I'm kidding. For me, to try to explain what drumming and rhythm is all about, well, it's beyond the mechanics. It's beyond the rudiments. It's beyond whether you lean a little this way or that way. It's beyond whether a guy plays Latin in 4/4—we call it "white Latin" if you're not playing it the way it's meant to be. It's all different variations. But underneath it all is the pulse, and beyond that is your own experience of what you're doing.

Christopher Otazo

If you're expressing yourself, it's bouncing back to the universe, so to speak—whether that's applause from an audience or your own satisfaction with what you did. That's what it's about. If you don't enjoy playing, then it becomes work. I love that line of Charlie Watts'. When asked how he was enjoying the tour, he said, "It's bloody hard work!"

MD: Is that how you feel?

Alex: In 1995, yes, but not this tour. When you have physical problems and you're trying to make it through without breaking, yes, it's hard work.

MD: Are there things you do now to make sure nothing breaks?

Alex: There are things I *don't* do anymore. [laughs]

MD: Is this a strong band or a fragile band? We hear stories about Eddie's health and temperament on the road, and his relationship with David Lee Roth….

Alex: None of it is true.

MD: So everything is solid and straight-ahead?

Alex: That's not true either. I preface everything by saying that we were in high school when we first got together. You put Ed, Dave, and me in a room, and one of us is going to come out bloody. And that's what makes it great. That element is still there. Music is an emotional thing. I'm not saying you need to be overbearing or disrespectful. But I am saying that our nature is such that we tend to overlap in how we get things done.

MD: And you're probably better at dealing with personalities within the band than in '85, when Roth left.

Alex: The biggest irony is that we're all on the same page. We're only trying to make things better. It reminds me of those infamous tapes you hear of Buddy Rich screaming at his band. He only wanted them to be better—that's all.

MD: Are you at all interested in keeping your double bass drum work on par with the drummers of today? Do you listen to some of the young double bass firebrands, like Joey Jordison, Chris Adler, or Jason Bittner?

Alex: I like a challenge, but to me it has to fit in with the music we're playing. Otherwise there's not much of a point to it. But strictly from a mechanical standpoint of someone being able to do that, I am impressed. Absolutely.

MD: But you're not concerned with trying to adapt that technique to Van Halen?

Alex: Not today. Though if I presented that to Ed he would write something based on that.

MD: Were you a big fan of John Bonham? Did you dissect his playing?

Alex: What I really liked is that Jimmy Page spent time to make the drum sound an integral part of the recording process. Ed and I have always been tone chasers. The sounds and the textures of sounds…that's what we've always tried to find.

MD: Your snare drum and bass drum sounds are unique.

Alex: That's part of it, but also how those sounds fit into the song. An extreme example would be "When the Levee Breaks." Led Zeppelin stumbled on that by accident. Andy Johns, who had recorded that song and also recorded one of our records, told me that Zeppelin were playing in the

hallway of Headley Grange. They had forgotten to turn on the close mics, and all they heard in the control room were the ambient mics, and it worked for the song. They always paid a lot of attention to the drums, and that's why those are some of the best-sounding records for drums.

Often on your earlier records, it's all on the clock. I still remember my first recording experience using a 26" bass drum and a 6.5" snare. The first thing the engineer asked me to do was remove the bottom tom heads and the front bass drum head. I was speechless. "You're out of your mind!" Ten minutes later, the drum heads were off. It took me until 5 P.M. to get the heads back on, and Ed helped me with it. It was a fight. Engineers have a certain way, their trip. But for me, you're asking me to take the sound out of my drums.

MD: How does that figure into your tuning on the tour?

Alex: We basically run everything flat.

> "You put Ed, Dave, and me in a room, and one of us is going to come out bloody. And that's what makes it great. That element is still there."

I don't want any EQ. We use Shure SM57s on the kick drums as well as a Shure Beta 91 to add some bottom if necessary. We use SM57s on the snares and Sennheiser clip-ons for the toms. Overheads are two AKG C414s and two Shure KSM32s.

MD: How do you direct your drum tech, Scott Oliver, to tune the kit?

Alex: We do an hour-long soundcheck for every gig. That's when I tune them up. As Buddy Rich would say, "You don't tune them, you tension them." In my bass drums, I want punch. If it gets too high-pitched, the bass drum will resonate too much. So I tune the bass drums to where it stops doing that. I use felt beaters because I can't take the chance of a wood beater going through a head during a show. But I use wood in the studio.

it. At the time we put the set together, the second drum tech, Johnny Douglas, had some input.

MD: How does this kit differ from your older ones?

Alex: This is the best-sounding kit I've ever had. It has fewer drums than some of my older kits. As for the sound of the kit out in the house, I depend on

the sweet spot. If you go too high, it'll sound like corn popping. Too low, and it won't sound good either.

Years ago engineers used to use a lot of tape on the drum to quiet the resonance, but not anymore. It became a problem because all the grace notes got lost. And it sounded like a box. You got that one note you liked, that crack.

Christopher Otazo

MD: Your double bass tour kit has extra bass drums attached to your main drums. Is that for sonics or looks?

Alex: The outer drums resonate. There's one big bass drum, joined to half of another bass drum. The smaller drum is attached to the main drum and it rings. It gives a more balanced sound.

I didn't want four bass drums, but I wanted more than two. This is my playground. If I want to make square drums, or use a hundred drums, I'll do

the soundman. Most of these guys just get a "tick" sound and low end. They save the rest of the frequency range for vocals, bass, and guitar. It's easier to mix. Wrong.

MD: Your snare drum has always sounded like a rocket.

Alex: That's a Ludwig wood drum. I've always played a Ludwig steel drum, but my drum tech brought in the wood snare one day and it sounded great. I don't tune it super tight; I find

But everything else? Nothing.

MD: Do you muffle the snare drum at all?

Alex: I run all of the drums wide open.

MD: You can hear that in the kick drums; they sound like canons. But how does that change in the studio?

Alex: It's all the same. And I play with the same volume and dynamics in the studio. When we record, it's like the Stones. They just start playing. If the third take is the right one, then that's the one. Ed and I just play until it feels comfortable.

For us, the recording experience is not outcome-driven. We're not looking to have anything at the end of the day. But at the end of the day we will have something.

MD: Are there any other drummers, old or new, who inspire your drumming today?

Alex: I listen to everybody. You gravitate to the old stuff that brings back the memories of your youth. But music is an ongoing thing; it's in constant flux.

MD: What's on your iPod?

Alex: What's an iPod? [laughs]

MD: Isn't it great that kids can have instant singles downloaded to their iPods?

Alex: I think it's destroyed the whole idea of having an album. To have a collection of songs that are somewhat connected, but not. The idea to

shambles, but a band like Van Halen can still sell out stadiums across the country. Perhaps people are hungry for that kind of band identity.

Alex: Eventually the pendulum will swing, but unfortunately everything is economically driven. When the intellectual property is threatened, then somebody will do something. The industry was looking the wrong way when it happened. And it doesn't do the artist any good. The artist is always the low man on the totem pole.

Our dad played in big bands, and when the big bands went down, a lot of people were out of work. I thought, "How does that affect me?" But now you have a similar thing happening. The good thing that will come out of it is that the people who really want to make music and understand the connection between music, people,

Anthony on bass?

Alex: I would never compare anybody to anybody.

MD: Why not?

Alex: Because there's always one winner and one loser, and that's not what it's all about. That's like comparing Dave Weckl to Vinnie Colaiuta. Dave is Dave and Vinnie is Vinnie. The only competition belongs in sports. But I gotta say, Wolfgang is an old soul. The guy has a groove you'll not believe. It's hard to hear in a live show, but you will when we make a record. Wolfgang is a player. It goes back to what Steve Smith said about defining the difference between time and pulse. The pulse now is so deep. I can't explain it, but you can feel it.

Eddie would tell you the same thing: If Wolfgang couldn't cut it—son or no son—he wouldn't be on the gig.

MD: Van Halen always played on the edge of the beat. Have you worked on ways to steady the time from the old days?

Alex: As I said earlier, we grew up on classical music, and we learned that when you need something to

"Because [Eddie and I] had a classical background, we knew that you use dynamics and rhythm changes to your advantage. The idea of trying to create strict metronomic time is nonsense."

have a cohesive piece of work to be representative of a certain period of your life, those things that have depth and add meaning to what you do, aren't there anymore. This is a disposable society and everything is a one-minute wonder. And that's unfortunate, because the next generation will do the same thing. Who do they have to learn from?

MD: The industry seems to be in

and the big picture will continue to do that.

In the '70s, when we were trying to get signed, we weren't in fashion. They wanted disco and punk. Twenty different labels turned us down. So we just played and put on our own shows, and we drew thousands of people. If you like playing, go out and play.

MD: How does the groove differ between having Wolfgang and Michael

propel the music and you only have two instruments, once you've used dynamics to take it to the next level, you give it a nudge. It won't hurt. Our time is elastic. As long as Ed and I are playing together, it's cool.

MD: Do you approach time any differently now?

Alex: If something needs a push, we push it. Like Vinnie said to me when I saw him on tour with Sting, "You guys always sound like you're chomping at the bit." And that's a good thing.

I'm the first to admit that I push the beat. But we're not there to recreate a song. We're there to put you on fire. We're there to get the audience involved with what we're doing. It's not a one-way street. The audience is part of it. But we're not looking backwards, we're looking forward.

MD: Do you have room to improvise during the shows?

Alex: Yes, but I don't want to clutter things up. We want the 2007 version of the songs that we played in 1984. We don't play them in the same way. That would be a disservice to us, and a disservice to the audience. We're not there to replay a record. This is who we are today, playing those songs that haven't been heard for twenty-three years. That's a long time for these songs to be sitting idle.

MD: Your solo at the Meadowlands combined three different themes, using double bass drum patterns and single-note rolls between your hands and bass drums.

Alex: I can't remember exactly what I played, though I am playing some single bass drum notes alternating with the floor tom. It's blocked out in three different sections. The first part is my tribute to Ginger Baker, my memory of when I first heard "Toad." My take on it is understandable. It's in 4/4, but the time flops. Baker was a master of that. My solo comes out of "Pretty Woman," and starting off with the Ginger idea just felt natural. If we'd come out of "Hot for Teacher," which was the original plan, I would have played something different. Everything is organic.

The second part of the solo is where I throw an old flanger on the drum sound. I do whatever I feel at the moment. Then it builds up and I do a tempo change from fast to slow to fast, which draws in the crowd. Then the last part is something taken from a Latin piece, comprised of the songs we didn't do live, like "Outta Love Again." I took little pieces of older songs and asked Steve Porcaro to orchestrate them. He put some NIN sounds in there, too. The part over the prerecorded track is all odd meter, using different stickings that I can't explain because I go by the melody. Even Steve had a little trouble because it's not in a straight meter.

MD: Finally, you mentioned earlier that you're a natural drummer. Does that really mean that you don't need to practice to stay on top of your game?

Alex: No, I have to practice. And I should have practiced more when the band first started. Steve Smith is very dedicated, and he has great insights. If I was just starting out, I would talk to Steve.

There's a certain camaraderie between musicians. We don't talk about it; nobody wants to know about the hours you've spent practicing in a closet—well, drummers do, but some people don't. But my main point is, in music, you can't do it alone. It's a team effort. I'm hanging around with guys I've known for thirty-five years. How many people have done that or even gotten along with somebody for that long? You can't do it alone.

Original interview by Ken Micallef

1978 Van Halen Tour Kit

The most obvious and visually striking element that Alex introduced when Van Halen appeared on the scene in 1978 was his long kick drums. Alex's right drum was a 14x26, and his left was a 14x24. Each of these had another drum of the same size added to it, making two double-length bass drums. This was done by removing the resonant heads from the primary drums and the batter heads from the auxiliary drums, and then connecting each pair. This was revolutionary: Nobody had done it before!

Alex stretched leather straps across the shells where they joined, hiding the seams. Chains were then strapped on top of that and connected to the deck of the drum riser, anchoring the drums to it like a wild beast that needed to be chained up to protect the world from it.

The other interesting element of this kit was the third rack tom placed in front of the mounted rack toms. This was a 14" Slingerland tom that was extra deep. It was placed in a snare stand and positioned between the 13" and 14" rack toms.

The insides of all of Alex's Silver Sparkle–finish shells were painted white. And quite often there was a gas mask hanging off the tom, further driving home the message, "These guys are dangerous!" As the tour progressed, Alex began to add black Tama Octobans to the setup.

Drums: Ludwig
- 28x26 bass drum (two 14x26 bass drums joined together)
- 28x24 bass drum (two 14x24 bass drums joined together)
- 9x13 and 10x14 toms
- 12x14 Slingerland tom
- 16x16 and 16x18 floor toms
- 6.5x14 Super Sensitive snare
- Tama Octobans (black)

Cymbals: Paiste 2002s, including 15" Sound Edge hi-hats, 18" and 20" crashes, a 20" China, and a 24" ride.

Neil Zlozower–Atlas Icons

Neil Zlozower/Atlas Icons

UMKITS

by John Douglas

Gear Notes

The best attempt was made to be as accurate as possible when gathering the information presented here. Unfortunately no one was contemporaneously documenting all the specifics (especially in the early days), and photo references sometimes make it very difficult to determine sizes and models, particularly in regard to cymbals. In addition, it was quite common for Alex to change things during the course of a tour, adding and removing drums and changing out cymbals.

It should be noted that Alex has only had four major endorsements his entire career, and he's been with those companies since the beginning—sometimes using their products years before an official endorsement was instituted. Those companies are Ludwig drums, Paiste cymbals, Regal Tip/Calato sticks, and Remo heads.

In regards to hardware, Alex has always used whatever meets his needs at the time. He's used many brands, most notably Ludwig, Tama, and DW. The bass drum pedals he's used the most are Ludwig's Speed King and Ghost models, the Yamaha Dragon, the Tama Iron Cobra, and, most recently, the Ludwig Atlas. And of course each kit always included an LP cowbell.

1979 Van Halen II Kit

The most obvious new element of the 1979 kit was the use of stainless-steel shells and clear Tama Octobans. Other additions included the outsides of each of the long kick drums being fitted with large chrome headers from a racing boat engine, as well as the employment of red shock absorbers as spurs. Since the shells were made of steel, the double kick drums were welded together, truly making for two extra-long shells.

A giant "Flammable" sticker was stuck on the side of the primary kick drum—and for good reason. At the end of every show, Alex would play with mallets that had been soaked in lighter fluid, and he would finish out the set fully engulfed in flames! Fire extinguishers became a staple at the drum riser, and also hung on the side of the left kick drum.

Because David Lee Roth had begun climbing on the kick drums, the shells had steel plates mounted to their top sections to strengthen them. Each bass drum also had two Tama Shell Supporters for added strength.

During the course of this tour, Alex added numbers on the outside of each drum as a joke: "Drumming by numbers." We also began to see Alex placing Octobans on the front of his kit. This became a theme that he would use to great effect in the coming years.

Neil Zlozower/ Atlas Icons

Neil Zlozower/ Atlas Icons

Drums: Ludwig Stainless Steel
• 28x26 bass drum (two 14x26 bass drums welded together)
• 28x24 bass drum (two 14x24 bass drums welded together)
• 9x13 and 10x14 toms
• 16x18 and 18x20 floor toms
• 6.5x14 Super Sensitive snare
• two clear 6" Tama Octobans in front of toms
• two 8" Octobans stage left and facing out, for Eddie Van Halen to play during "Light Up the Sky"
• four 8" Octobans over the floor toms

Cymbals: Paiste 2002s, including 15" Sound Edge hi-hats, 18", 19", and 20" crashes, a 20" medium crash, a 24" Power ride, and a 20" China

1980 Women and Children First Kit

This kit featured another new, visually striking element: articulating kick drums, which began a long fascination Alex had with flexible hoses joining drums. Rather than the double-length bass drum shells being joined together at the bearing edges, as on the '78 and '79 kits, Alex started with single-headed bass drum shells, then added flexible hoses that connected to the front drum shells, resulting in the kick drums that were more than 50" (!) deep.

The drums featured white Cortex maple shells with black-painted insides. All the toms were single-headed, like those of most arena-rock bands of the time.

This is the first time we see Alex using Pearl Vari-Pitch toms over his floor toms, essentially Rototoms mounted inside shells. This tour also introduced what was to become a staple on every subsequent Alex Van Halen drum riser: a 40" Paiste gong.

Neil Zlozower/ Atlas Icons

Neil Zlozower/ Atlas Icons

Drums: Ludwig
- 50x26 articulating bass drum
- 50x24 articulating bass drum
- 8x12, 9x13, and 10x14 toms
- 16x18 and 18x20 floor toms
- 6.5x14 Super Sensitive snare
- 12x10 Tama single-headed tom
- two 6" Tama Octobans
- 14" and 16" Pearl Vari-Pitch toms

Cymbals: Paiste 2002s, including 15"
Sound Edge hi-hats, 19" and 20" crashes
and mediums, a 24" heavy ride, a 20"
China, and a 40" Symphonic gong

1981 Fair Warning Kit

This is arguably Alex Van Halen's most iconic drumkit. The vertical black-and-white-striped Vistalite shells were a stock finish, but will forever be known as the Alex Van Halen Fair Warning finish. The insides of all the shells were reinforced with a 1/4" of fiberglass for strength and then painted white.

We also see the next advancement of AVH bass drum evolution: the addition of auxiliary bass drums. To the left and right of his primary, extra-long bass drums are 24" kicks connected to them with…what else…flexible hose! Alex was further experimenting with resonance, porting the sides of the kick drums, sending soundwaves into the auxiliary drums via ductwork. And the visual result was over-the-top.

Once again, all the toms are double-headed models with the bottom heads and hoops removed. This is also when we first see the use of the famous Tama Rosewood snare drum.

Neil Zlozower / Atlas Icons

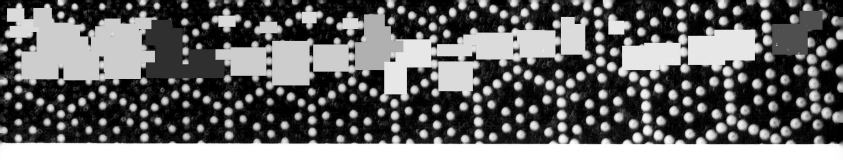

Neil Zlozower/ Atlas Icons

Drums: Ludwig Vistalite
• 6.5x14 Ludwig Super Sensitive or Tama Rosewood snare
• 28x26 bass drum
• 28x24 bass drum
• two 14x24 bass drums
• 8x8, 8x10, 8x12, 9x13, 10x14, 12x14, 11x15, and 12x16 toms
• 16x18 and 18x20 floor toms
• two 8" clear Tama Octobans

Cymbals: Paiste 2002s, including 15" Sound Edge hi-hats, 20" crashes, 19" and 20" mediums, a 24" Power ride, a 20" China, and a 40" Symphonic gong

THE DRUMKITS

1982 Diver Down Kit

Yet another development in kick drum visuals and sonic experimentation. After thinking about how a pipe organ employs different lengths of tubing to achieve relative pitches, Alex thought, "What if I did that with my kick drums, and miked whichever tube had the best sound in that particular room?" Starting with the by-now usual extra-long 26" and 24" kick drums, he replaced the front resonant heads with pipes of various lengths and diameters, cut at a 45-degree angle at their ends.

The overall color scheme of this kit was the opposite of what we saw on the 1980 kit. This time it was Black Cortex wrap on the outside of the drums and white paint inside. Once again, all toms were double-headed with the bottom heads and hoops removed, revealing their stark white insides.

Alex had a set of Ludwig timbales mounted on top of the stage-left auxiliary bass drum. These were used by Eddie during the set. In addition, Alex began the tour with 8" and 10" toms mounted over the stage-left kick drum (like the Fair Warning kit) but seems to have quickly taken them away, as most photos do not show them.

Notably, this is the first time we see Alex using the (at the time) latest technology in electronic drums, the Simmons SDS-V, with two or three pads placed over his floor toms. It's also where we begin to see the Paiste Rude models introduced into his cymbal setup.

Neil Zlozower/ Atlas Icons

Neil Zlozower / Atlas Icons

Drums: Ludwig
• 28x26 bass drum
• 28x24 bass drum
• two 16x20 auxiliary bass drums attached to the primary kicks via flexible hose
• 8x8, 8x10, 8x12, 9x13, and 10x14 toms
• 16x18 and 18x20 floor toms
• 6.5x14 Tama Rosewood snare
• 14" and 16" Pearl Vari-Pitch toms
• 13" and 14" Ludwig timbales, painted black

Electronics: Simmons SDS-V brain and pads

Cymbals: Paiste 2002s, including 15" Sound Edge hi-hats, 19" and 20" crashes and mediums, a 24" Power ride, and a 20" China, 24" Rude ride, 40" Paiste Symphonic gong

1983 Us Festival Kit

This was Van Halen's biggest gig up until this time, so it got an equally impressive drumkit, one that was only used on this show. Here we see the next progression of bass drum enhancements. The volume on the Van Halen stage was so loud that Alex installed radial horns in his kick drums to boost the volume and enhance the attack while simultaneously creating a whole new look that matched the uniqueness of his playing style.

This was also the first time Alex had any kind of artwork applied to his drum finish, in this case stickers of a woman's mouth with bright red lipstick, which he plastered all over the kit himself. All the shells were painted white on the inside. This is also the debut of power toms on Alex's set.

Rick Malkin

Neil Zlozower/ Atlas Icons

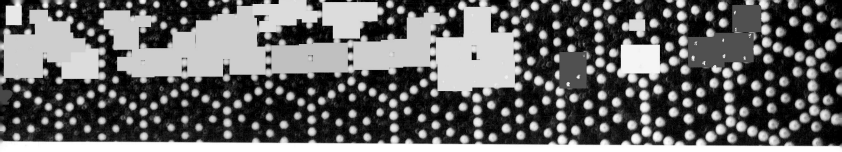

Drums: Ludwig
• 28x26 bass drum
• 28x24 bass drum
• 16x24 auxiliary kick drum connected to left main bass drum via flexible hose
• 10x12, 11x13, and 12x14 toms
• 16x18 and 18x20 floor toms
• 6.5x14 Tama Rosewood snare
• 14" and 16" Pearl Vari-Pitch toms

Electronics: Simmons SDS-V brain and pads

Cymbals: Paiste 2002s and Rudes, including 15" Sound Edge hi-hats (2002 top/Rude bottom), 20" mediums, 18" and 20" Rudes, a 24" Rude ride, a 20" 2002 China, and a 40" Symphonic gong

1984 Kit

The 1984 tour brought another legendary AVH kit. Once again we have the bass drums with radial horns mounted inside, but this time they're accented by a row of Tama Octobans covered in mirrored squares, as were the floor toms and Vari-Pitch toms. The bass drums had plywood mounted on their batter sides, with mounted triggers that were connected to the Simmons SDS V brain. This kit was another big artistic statement, and a landmark in rock 'n' roll excess.

Neil Zlozower/Atlas Icons

While the *1984* album and the video for its hit song "Jump" (left) both featured Rototoms, the tour-kit "toms" were Simmons SDS-V pads hidden behind the row of Octobans.

Neil Zlozower / Atlas Icons

Drums: Ludwig
• 28x26 bass drum
• 28x24 bass drum
• two 14x24 auxiliary bass drums attached to main
  bass drums via flexible ducts
• seven 6" Tama Octobans
• 16x18 and 18x20 floor toms
• 14" and 16" Pearl Vari-Pitch toms
• 6.5x14 Tama Rosewood snare

Electronics: Simmons SDS-V with five or
six pads

Cymbals: Paiste, including: 15" 2002 Sound
Edge hi-hats, 19" and 20" 2002 crashes and
mediums, a 24" 2002 Power ride, two 20"
2002 Chinas, and a 40" Symphonic gong

1986 5150 Kit

For the 5150 tour, Alex returned with the Altec radial horns mounted in his bass drums. This time, though, all the drums were clear Ludwig Vistalites in custom sizes, with astounding 1/2"-thick shells. Clear Tama Octobans were again positioned in front of Simmons tom pads, while the auxiliary bass drums were linked to the main ones via red hoses.

Drums: Ludwig Vistalites
• 28x26 bass drum
• 28x24 bass drum
• 14x26 auxiliary bass drum
• 14x24 auxiliary bass drum
• two 16x18 Vistalite floor toms
• 6.5x14 Tama Rosewood snare drum
• eight 6" clear Tama Octobans

Electronics: Simmons SDS-V pads

Cymbals: Paiste 2002s, 15" Sound Edge hi-hats, 19" and 20" crashes, mediums, and Power crashes, 24" Power ride, and 40" Paiste Symphonic gong

Ebet Roberts

1988
OU812/Monsters of Rock Kit

This was the Mother Ship of all AVH drumkits, set up in the round and on a rotating and elevating riser. Essentially the setup consisted of three different kits: one with Ludwig power toms, one with Tama Octobans fitted with Dauz pads that triggered a Simmons SDS-X brain, and one with North toms. There was a total of six bass drums, each with a radial horn mounted inside it. All of the drums had white finishes, with the exception of the clear Octobans, and everything was mounted on a custom-made single-piece 360-degree rack, with a gap for Alex to walk through.

Drums: Ludwig
• six 28x22 bass drums
• 10x10, 11x12, and 12x13 toms
• 16x16 floor tom
• 6", 8", 10", and 12" North toms
• 14" North floor tom
• 6" clear Tama Octobans
• three Tama Rosewood snares (6.5x14 and 8x14 models) painted white

Cymbals: Paiste 2002s, including three sets of 15" Sound Edge hi-hats, three 24" Power rides, 19" and 20" crashes, and 19" and 20" mediums, and a 40" Symphonic gong

Eddie Malluk/Atlas Icons

1991
For Unlawful Carnal Knowledge Kit

The six-piece, chrome-finish kit assembled for the For Unlawful Carnal Knowledge tour was very small by AVH standards. The toms and cymbal stands were attached to a simple rack system, and the single bass drum had chrome pipes bent at a 90-degree angle coming out of either side and into the riser.

Drums: Ludwig
- 20x22 bass drum
- 8x10 and 8x12 toms
- 16x16 and 16x18 floor toms
- 6.5x14 hammered bronze snare

Cymbals: Paiste, including 15" Signature Heavy Sound Edge hi-hats, 19" and 20" 2002 and Signature crashes, 19" and 20" 2002 and Signature mediums, a 22" Signature heavy ride, a 20" 2002 China, and a 40" Symphonic gong

1995 Balance Kit

Alex started the Balance tour with a Ludwig kit in green stain, but switched to one with a mahogany stain. To his left he'd set up a pair of LP congas, a pair of LP timbales, and four Tama Octobans painted to match the drums. Like with Alex's previous setup, the drums were mounted on a rack custom-built by Greg Voelker.

Drums: Ludwig
• two 16x24 bass drums
• 8x10 and 8x12 toms
• 16x16 and 16x18 floor toms
• 6.5x14 chrome-plated hammered-bronze snare
• four Tama 6" Octobans
• 14" and 15" LP brass timbales
• a pair of LP congas

Cymbals: Paiste, including 15" 2002 or Signature Sound Edge hi-hats, 18", 19", and 20" 2002 and Signature crashes, a 22" Signature heavy ride, a 12" 2002 heavy bell, and a 40" Paiste gong

THE DRUMKITS

1998 Van Halen III Kit

Alex's kit for the Van Halen III tour was very similar to the Balance tour kit. This time it was custom-painted bright yellow by drum tech John Douglas, with black hand-painted text of the words "Van Halen" in Sanskrit. The drums were attached to the Voelker rack from the previous tour. A pair of LP congas custom-painted with matching graphics were set up to Alex's left.

John Douglas

Drums: Ludwig Classic Maple
• two 16x24 bass drums
• 8x10 and 8x12 toms
• 16x16 and 16x18 floor toms
• 6.5x14 chrome-plated hammered-bronze Super Sensitive snare
• a pair of LP congas

Cymbals: Paiste, including hi-hats made up of a 15" Signature heavy top and a 14" 2002 Sound Edge bottom, 18", 19", and 20" 2002 and Signature crashes, a 20" Signature Mellow ride, a 12" 2002 bell, and a 40" Symphonic gong

The Elusive Alex Van Halen Snare Sound

by John Douglas

"How do I get my snare drum to sound like Alex Van Halen?" That question has crossed many drummers' minds ever since Van Halen burst onto the scene in 1978.

I'd received countless emails asking different variations of the same question. Everyone wants to know what exact equipment Alex plays to get *that* sound. You know the sound the minute you hear it—we all do. It's instantly identifiable. It puts the rocket in the pocket that drives one of the biggest and most successful rock bands of all time, the mighty Van Halen.

So what *is* the secret to the Alex Van Halen snare sound? I'll give away the secret right here, right now—but first a bit of history.

In all the years of my working with Alex, he's played a multitude of snare drums, with many different head combinations. It's well known that he favored a Tama Rosewood snare drum for many years, mainly in a 6.5" depth but also an 8" for a while. When I started with Alex he was using a Ludwig hammered-bronze Super Sensitive with die-cast hoops and a Ludwig Silver Dot batter head, which had the legendary, unconventional gaffer's tape application on its underside. On that particular drum I had to fashion a carburetor return spring onto its throw-off, as it would tend to disengage during a performance. The spring kept the throw-off in the "on" position—it could still be turned off, but it just took a bit more force.

I've watched Alex play many different Ludwig snares in addition to the hammered-bronze Super Sensitive, including a Hammered Brass, a Classic Maple, and the most recorded drum in history, the Supraphonic. He's also tried a fiberglass snare and a carbon-fiber snare. And naturally he played his first Ludwig signature snare, which was made of rosewood. More recently he's played his second signature snare, the artistically modified Ludwig Supraphonic featuring copper-plated hardware, tube lugs, die-cast hoops, and forty-strand snare wires.

Wait, what? He used *all* those different drums, but still got the magic AVH sound every time? Okay, then maybe it's a special drumhead combination, or a secret muffling technique. Well, Alex has used an exhausting number of drumhead combinations on all of these drums—Ludwig Silver Dot…Ludwig Heavy…Remo Black Dot, Emperor Coated, and Pinstripe models. Eventually he even moved away from the gaffer's tape and settled on a Remo Emperor X on the batter side and an Ambassador snare-side.

How about Alex's tuning—perhaps there's something unique he does? Well, for starters, Alex's batter head is not tuned as high as most people think—it's cranked enough to give him the crack he's looking for, but not so tight that there's no body, no meat on the backbeat. Same with the bottom head: not too tight. And there's no special detuning of certain tension rods either; equal tension is applied all around on both heads. And the snare wires are a bit loose, so that the drum doesn't choke on the loudest hits.

Maybe the secret to Alex's elusive sound is in his drumstick. Sorry to disappoint you, but he changes his stick models almost every tour, sometimes even mid-tour. Alex started with massive 2S marching sticks and ultimately landed on his Regal Tip signature stick, which is .57" round and an astounding 17.75" long. He's played that stick in a special double-butt version; he's played the same-diameter double-butt version only an inch shorter—on one tour, on any given day I could be found backstage cutting an inch off the back end of his sticks. Lately he's been playing a stick that's .635" in diameter by 17" long.

Of course, the way Alex strikes the drum is crucial to the sound. A consistent rimshot is what it's all about. And where that stick lands plays an important role, and not only the location on the batter head (slightly off center) but also how much of the stick makes contact with the head and where the stick meets the rim.

Too many variations, diameters, lengths, weights, and tips have been tried and tested for me to document here. Suffice it to say that Alex, like his brother Eddie, is a constant tone chaser. Always searching and experimenting while honing his craft.

All these various combinations of shell material, drumheads, muffling techniques, and different stick models, and Alex Van Halen always sounds like Alex Van Halen. Whether in a studio or in a stadium, he's always achieved that instantly recognizable *crack*. So what's the secret?

Here's my conclusion: The secret to achieving Alex's sound is…you have to *be* Alex Van Halen. It's that simple.

During the course of a tour I'm privileged to get to play his drums, tuning them and getting them ready for the band to soundcheck. When I play his drums, it sounds like me (which is very frustrating!), and when Alex sits down and plays the same kit, in the same room, it sounds like him. Magic.

What I've learned is this: It's not so much the gear—it's the guy hitting that gear.

2004
Best of Both Worlds Kit

This tour featured a Ludwig Classic Maple kit in natural finish and the return of tube drums, this time 8" clear models custom-made by Pork Pie Percussion with custom dragon art etched into them. Dauz pads replaced their batter heads, triggering a ddrum 4 brain loaded with custom samples. Four of these were set up above a piccolo snare drum to the left of Alex's hi-hat, while two more were placed above his floor toms. Drums and cymbals were mounted on a custom-made rack designed and fabricated by drum tech John Douglas and Rick Grossman. A unique dragon was also hand-painted onto each of the three front bass drum heads by Douglas, as was Alex's main snare drum. Coil-over shock absorbers were added to each kick drum as a nod to his 1979 kit.

John Douglas

John Douglas

Drums: Ludwig Classic Maple in natural finish
- two 14x26 bass drums
- 16x24 bass drum
- 8x12 and 9x13 toms
- 16x16 and 16x18 floor toms
- 6.5x14 chrome hammered-bronze Supraphonic snare
- 3x13 Black Beauty piccolo snare
- eight clear Pork Pie 8" tube drums

Cymbals: Paiste 2002s, including 15" Sound Edge hi-hats, 18", 19", and 20" mediums and crashes, a 22" Power ride, and a 40" Symphonic gong

2007-2008
North American Tour Kit

The 2007–2008 tour saw the return of David Lee Roth—and of bass drum resonance experimentation. This time each of the 16x26 main kicks had an additional 22" shell attached to it in a unique fashion: a section was cut out so that it nestled next to the main shell, "sharing" its resonance. The resonance kicks also had chrome heat sinks protruding out of their shells. The look, of course, was out of this world. The drums' finish was an ice blue flake, custom-painted by John Douglas over black Ludwig Classic Maple shells. This kit also featured the now legendary "fridge kick," a 24" bass drum that had a working refrigerator inside, accessible via a door installed onto the front head.

John Douglas

John Douglas

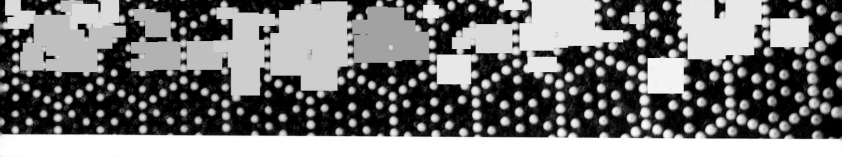

John Douglas

Drums: Ludwig Classic Maple
• two 16x26 bass drums (with custom "side-port" drums)
• 16x24 bass drum (with working refrigerator mounted inside)
• 8x12 and 9x13 toms
• 16x16 and 16x18 floor toms
• 6.5x14 maple main snare
• 4x13 Black Beauty piccolo snare
• eight 8" custom-built Pork Pie tube drums with Dauz pads mounted inside

Cymbals: Paiste, including 15" 2002 Sound Edge hi-hats, 19", 20", and 22" 2002 crashes, a 24" Giant Beat ride, a 20" 2002 China, and a 38" Symphonic gong

2012
A Different Kind of Truth Kit

Perhaps the most distinguishing feature of this kit is the return to the long bass drums—albeit with a slightly different approach. Alex likes his kick drums only muffled with a felt strip and with no holes in their resonant heads. On this kit, the bass drums placed in front act as isolation cabinets for mics aimed at the resonant heads of the drums behind them. The kit also had two auxiliary bass drums on each side with beer pulls mounted on the front.

The finish of this set is a custom engine-turned metal accented with brass hardware. Alex also added a second set of hi-hats on a DW remote stand, a pair of Taye timbales, and four Tama Octobans. Everything was mounted on a custom rack using DW components.

Mark Weiss

Mark Weiss

Drums: Ludwig Classic Maple
- two 16x26 bass drums with 14x26 drums attached in front
- two 18x20 auxiliary bass drums
- 8x12 and 9x13 toms
- 16x16 and 16x18 floor toms
- 6.5x14 matching snare (On tour, Alex used a ground-metal Supraphonic model, which would become the prototype for his Signature snare.)
- four Tama 6" Octobans
- 12" and 13" Taye stainless-steel timbales

Cymbals: Paiste 2002s, including two pairs of 15" Sound Edge hi-hats, 19", 20", and 22" crashes and mediums, a 24" Reverend Al's Big Ride, a 20" China, and a 50" Symphonic gong

2015 North American Tour Kit

This kit has been called "the logo kit" by drum tech John Douglas, who says, "We set out to put the classic VH logo whereever we could—tastefully or semi-tastefully!" A striking chrome wrap was offset by custom copper-plated hardware and covered with custom artwork featuring the VH logo. Special badges were cast in copper combining the VH logo with the Ludwig Keystone, honoring Alex's forty-year anniversary with the drum maker. Each Paiste cymbal had the VH logo imprinted on it as well, and Remo printed the logo on each drumhead. The bass drum heads had the logo done in a stealth matte black on gloss black. Custom Pork Pie 8" tube drums complete the kit.

Drums: Ludwig Classic Maple
- two 14x26 bass drums with 14x26 drums attached in front
- two 18x20 auxiliary bass drums
- 8x12 and 9x13 toms
- 16x16 and 16x18 floor toms
- 6.5x14 Ludwig Supraphonic (prototype for the AVH Signature snare)
- three 8" Pork Pie maple tube drums
- 12" and 13" Taye stainless-steel timbales

Cymbals: Paiste 2002s, including 15" Sound Edge hi-hats, 19", 20", and 22" crashes and mediums, a 24" Reverend Al's Big Ride, a 20" China, and a 50" Symphonic gong

Marco Soccoli

THE SONGS

"Dance the Night Away" (II)

This classic cowbell groove kicks off the intro of "Dance the Night Away."

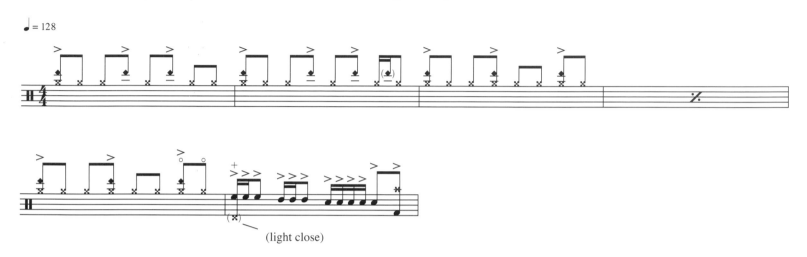

Alex leaves space at the beginning of the pre-chorus before the band plays unison accents on beats 2 and 3. He mutes the crash cymbals to make room for his fills to articulate with the vocals.

[Regarding the cowbells] "The producer, Ted Templeman, asked me to do some Stones 'Honky Tonk Women' thing at the beginning. It was a vibe. It's funny—I didn't like that song at all. [laughs] We were opening up for Black Sabbath, and they came out with [Alex sings Sabbath-y riff], and they made the walls crack. And here we are, playing 'Dance the Night Away'...oh, f**k me. [laughs] Years later, of course, it's a great tune and it was well-written and people like it. And that's ultimately the gauge. You're not there for you; you're there for the audience."

"Jump" (1984)

On the pre-chorus of "Jump," Alex phrases across the vocal melody with a three-note grouping that alternates between the bell of the ride cymbal, the hi-hat, and the snare drum. He syncs up with the guitar melody before delivering a no-nonsense fill that leads into the chorus.

[Regarding the drums during the guitar solo] "The tendency would have been to really go over the top. Just to go bonkers. Ed kept saying we shouldn't do that. We instinctively knew if we did, the song would not get any airplay. Do the crazy shit on tour, afterwards. There were a couple of times where I wanted to do something off, maybe a beat reversal, put it upside down for a split second, but why risk it when we were in the middle of a good take? I wanted to do something like the blushda in there, but between the toms and the feet, but I realized, I better not f**k everything up. [laughs] But live, we would go apeshit. But there, you're limited because Dave never knows where the 1 is. [laughs] In the spirit of being a unit, you don't want to impress the other guys and throw them off.

Alex pulls the rug out from under the listener during the guitar solo by dislocating the driving backbeat. The kick, snare, and ride dance around the keyboard background parts through Eddie's shredding solo. He switches gears and straightens out the groove through the keyboard arpeggios, grabbing onto the quarter-note triplets to conclude the section.

"Panama" (1984)

The beginning of "Panama" can immediately deceive the ear, as the first note starts on the "and" of beat 1. Alex plays a bumpy rhythm on the toms that lands accents in the gaps of Eddie's guitar riff. The four-on-the-floor groove that follows is a great example of Alex's mighty forward momentum inside of the pocket.

Alex sets up the offbeat guitar rhythms in the pre-chorus like a big band drummer by playing fills in the spaces.

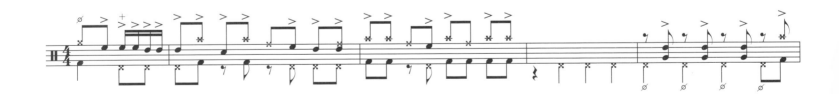

He spices things up in the guitar solo by adding some quick triple beats on the ride cymbal.

[Regarding the tom-heavy intro]
"More jungle! In my mind, there's nothing worse than playing in unison. The way I was taught was when Ed plays a certain rhythm, you have to dance around it. Do the other thing; make it what it isn't and make it move. If you notice, I don't play with Ed. And if you listen to later live recordings, I play it the way it should have been done on the record. The Simmons really were a problem."

"Hot for Teacher" (1984)

The song "Hot for Teacher" has one of the most famous drum intros of all time. The hertas at the beginning are played on a Simmons pad, followed by the bass drums coming in underneath with a fast shuffle rhythm. The low rumble of the punchy kicks and toms are reminiscent of an idling motorcycle. Alex adds another layer of interest by throwing in some over-the-barline tom accents on top. When he breaks into the groove, he plays an inverted swing rhythm on the ride bell that fills in the first two notes of the triplet.

Note: The bass drums are notated left-foot lead but can be played however you are comfortable. Feel free to experiment.

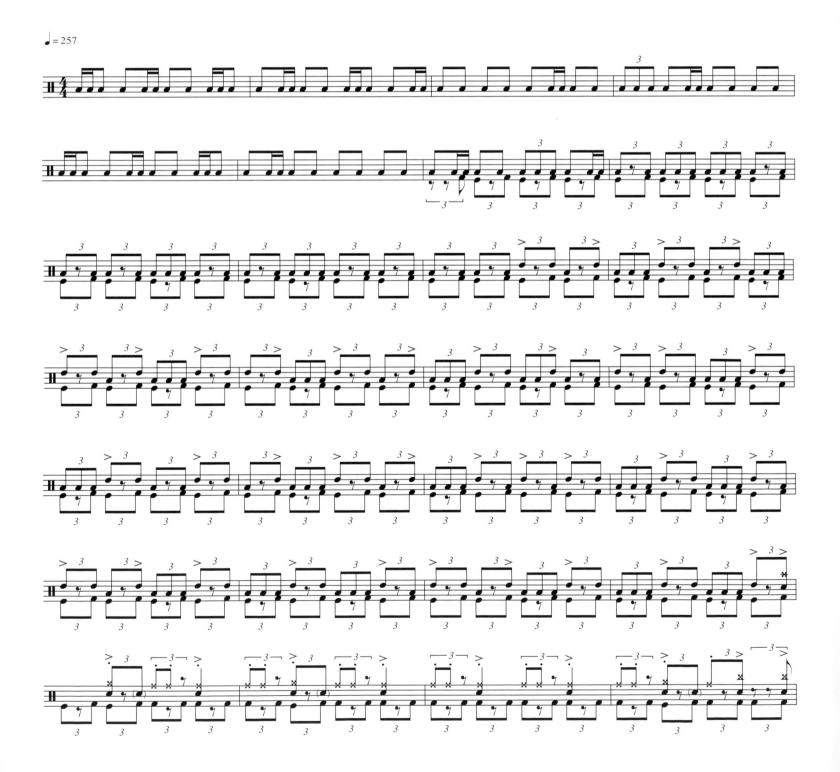

"'Hot for Teacher' happened very fast. Ed, Mike, and I were playing, and there it was. I was a big fan of Billy Cobham, and Ed really got off on Mahavishnu Orchestra. So that was our tip of the hat, if you will. [There were] a lot of little Ed licks, these rhythmic things he did, and I mirrored them maybe eight bars later. When you play the second verse, don't play it the same; do something different. So with my little fills, there was just enough room to squeeze them in without stepping on Ed. You don't want to step on the guitar. Making music is like, You're talking, I'm talking—we're having a conversation. But please don't talk while I'm talking." [laughs]

Alex plays some exciting lead-in fills coming out of the guitar breakdown riffs. This one utilizes bass drum ruffs to lead into an accent on the "and" of 4.

The pre-chorus has lots of upbeat guitar accents that Alex catches on the snare drum and cymbals while the kick drums shuffle underneath.

The fill after the second breakdown ascends up the toms and contorts the rhythm with straight 8th notes.

Straight 8th notes

The third breakdown fill plays off the same theme as the first, but the orchestration changes to add variety.

"Dreams" (5150)

Here is a tasteful kick drum fill at the end of the second verse of "Dreams" that goes against the rhythm of Eddie's keyboard accents.

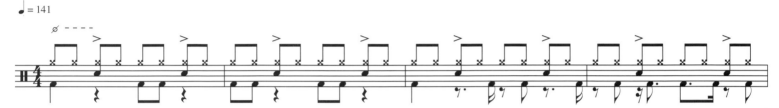

This herta fill really ratchets up the excitement going into the guitar solo.

The kick drums roll into the big accents at the end of the solo section.

Alex plays a great double bass/snare drum combination that leads to the outro.

[Regarding the Simmons sound of the record] "Human beings tend to group and travel together through different changes. If you can weather those changes and not compromise what you do, and have the influences enter what you're doing, then you're all right. Because of the success of 'Jump' and the singer change, the keyboard tunes became more prominent. And remember, Ed and I started off on keyboards. The irony is the two biggest hits this band ever had ["Jump" and "Why Can't This Be Love"] were keyboard tunes. I wasn't unhappy with the Simmons drums, but I wasn't super happy either. It's a one-dimensional sound. It's not as livable and breathable as a real drum. But it got the job done, and I'm certainly not embarrassed with what we did."

"Right Now" (*For Unlawful Carnal Knowledge*)

"Right Now" features quite a few rhythmic twists. The piano part starts on the "e" of count 1 and provides no concrete reference to where the downbeat lands. The unison accents on the bass, piano, and guitar come in on the "e" of 1 as well, so if you're not paying close attention, your ear can be hearing the 1 in the wrong place.

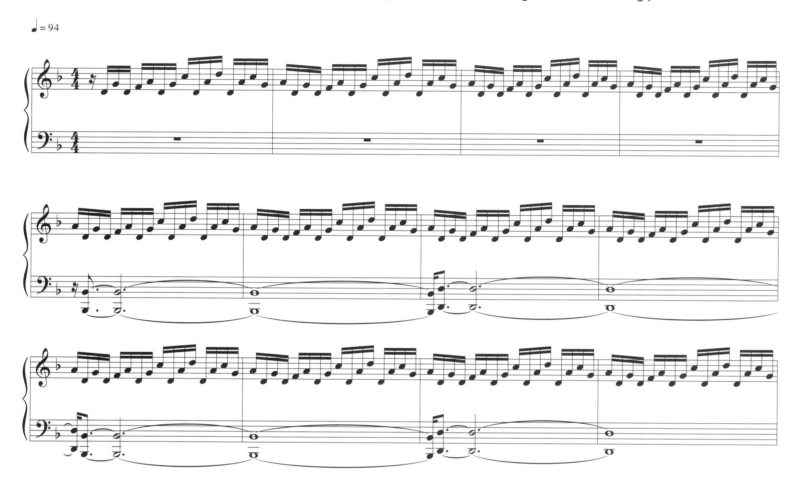

Alex's playing on this song is a real tour de force, as many of his great attributes are on display. The classic ride bell through the chorus, the backward tom fills, and the ultra funky verse groove are great examples of his approach. Check out how he leaves lots of space for Michael Anthony to play his bass lines in the verse, while creating forward motion with the 16th notes on the hi-hat.

"Right Now" continued

"Usually Ed and I start the process and figure out what sits right and what doesn't. It was just piano and drums, like Lee Michaels and Frosty, which creates an interesting dynamic because you don't have all those other instruments filling shit in. So you try to imagine how you would play this if it was just the two of you. And we added the other stuff later. If two of you can make it work well, then you've got it, and all you need is a chorus."

"I'm the One" (Van Halen)

The blazing tempo of "I'm the One" is the perfect vehicle for Alex to crank up his signature double bass shuffle. This amazing performance is a clinic on stamina, grit, and crisp execution of ideas. He brings his dynamics down to a whisper on the vocal breakdown after the guitar solo without losing the intensity before crescendoing into the ending tag.

Note: The bass drum pattern is notated right-foot lead, but other approaches can be applied. Experiment with what is most comfortable for you.

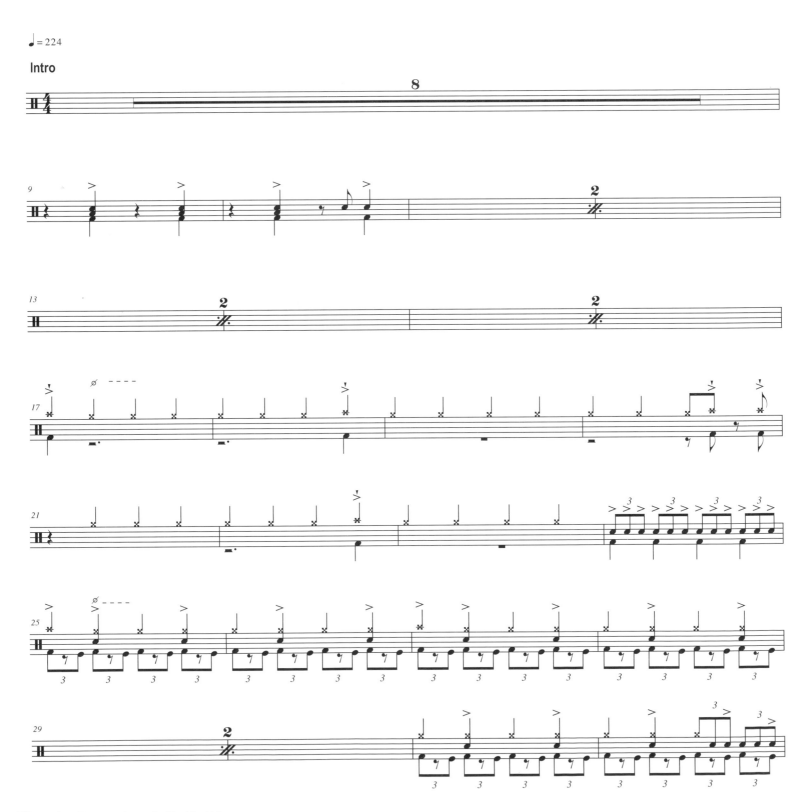

Verse

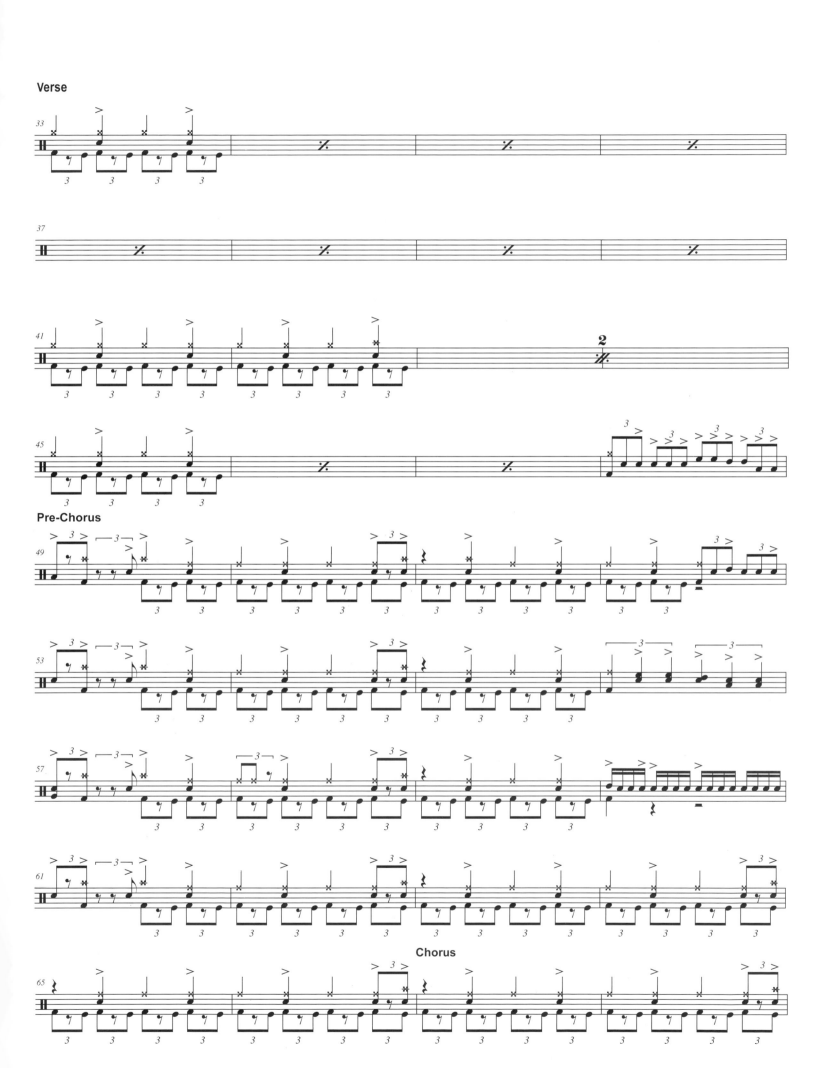

"I'm the One" continued

Guitar Solo

Vers

Pre-Chorus

it was good. That's part of the reason why there was conflict and there was creativity. Every one of us brought something different to the table."

"I'm the One" continued

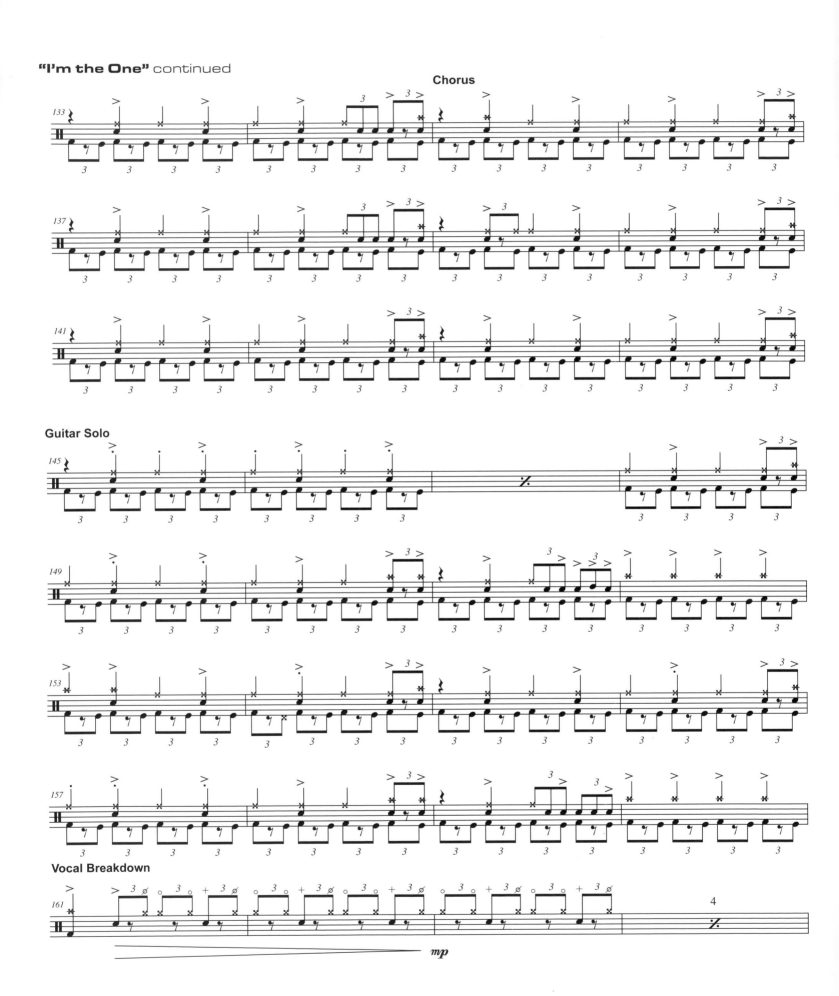

"Outta Love Again" (*II*)

The aggressive funk/fusion groove on "Outta Love Again" demonstrates Alex's fine control over his left-foot hi-hat pedaling. The left-hand ghost notes seamlessly blend in with his right-hand hi-hat notes.

Alex throws down some fast fills inside of the guitar accents on the chorus. The 3/4 measure on bar 5 turns the beat upside down.

A minimalistic two-note fill breaks the action before the raucous guitar solo section. The articulate bell patterns on the ride cymbal complement Eddie's playing.

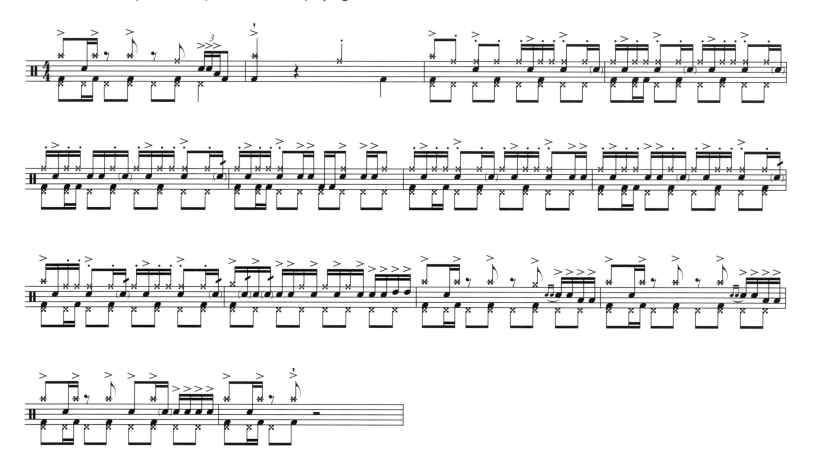

"We just wanted to do some funk without insulting the real funk guys and making something out of it. We weren't pretending to be anything. There are no rules. Count Basie said, 'If it sounds good, it is good.'"

"Loss of Control" (Women and Children First)

"Loss of Control" is a breakneck-speed double-time rocker that has Alex on his "A" game. He pummels through the intro with a fast double bass groove and settles into a hi-hat shout beat after the break.

Alex plays some Latin-inspired ride bell rhythms over the double bass/snare groove in the guitar solo.

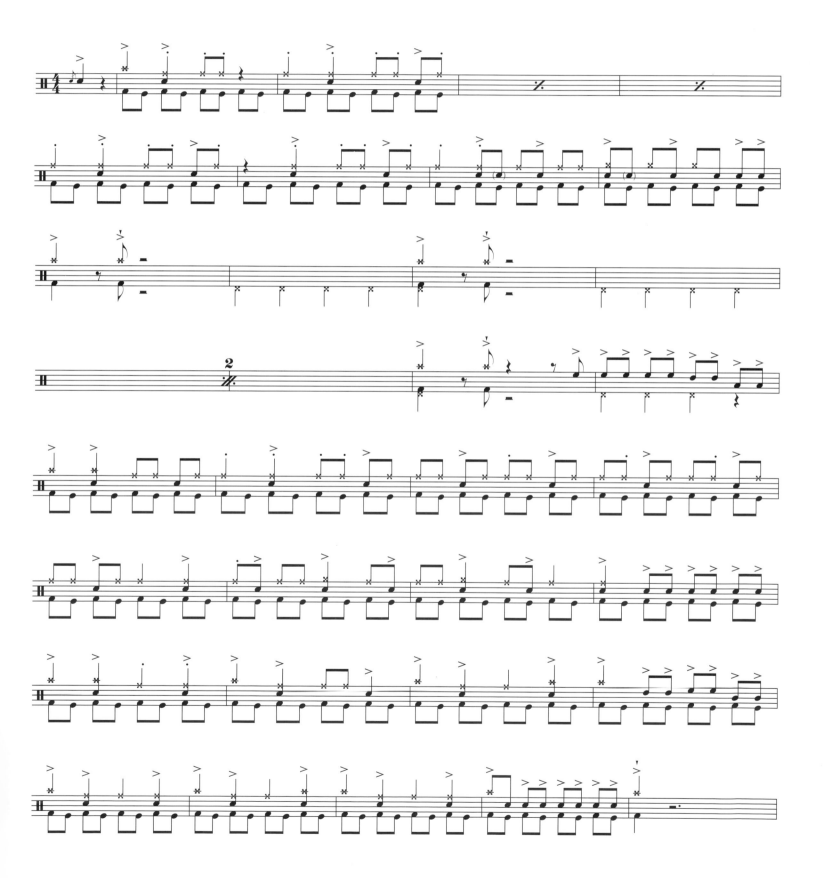

At the end of the song, Alex nails all of the accents with the band and brings the song in for a safe landing.

"To do it in the studio one time is great, but to have to do it every night, oh man! [laughs] It's one of the few times when you think to yourself, Maybe I should have played bass. We enjoyed going out to the edge—the old expression, 'You should go out on a limb; that's where the fruit is.'"

"Mean Street" (*Fair Warning*)

"Mean Street" shines a light on Alex and Michael Anthony's tight rhythm section playing. The bass drum chugs away at the upbeats while the hi-hat plays fast one-handed 16ths.

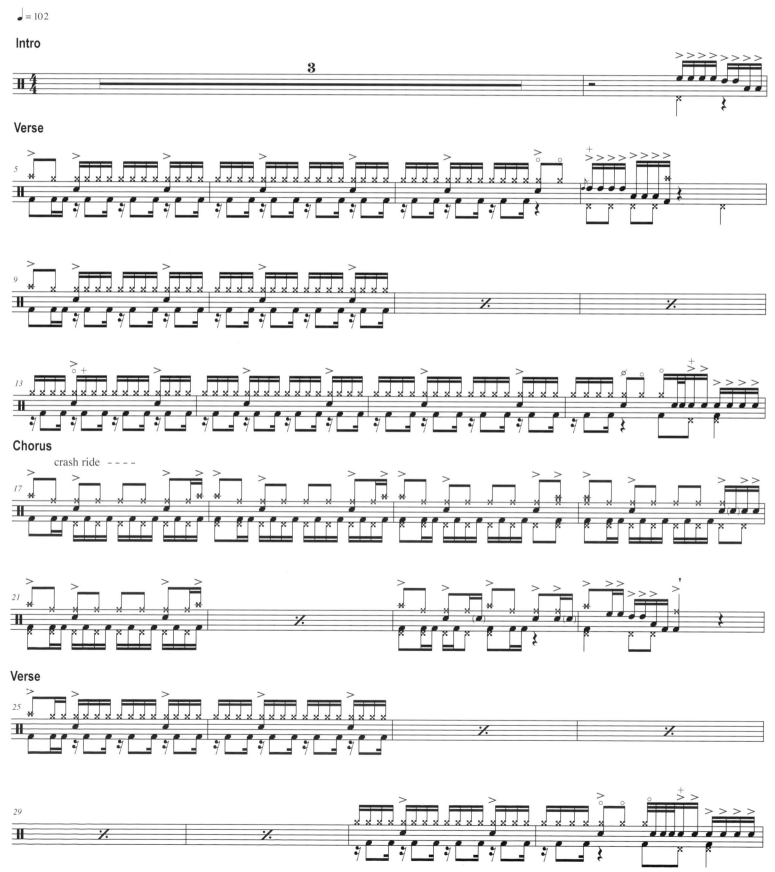

Chorus

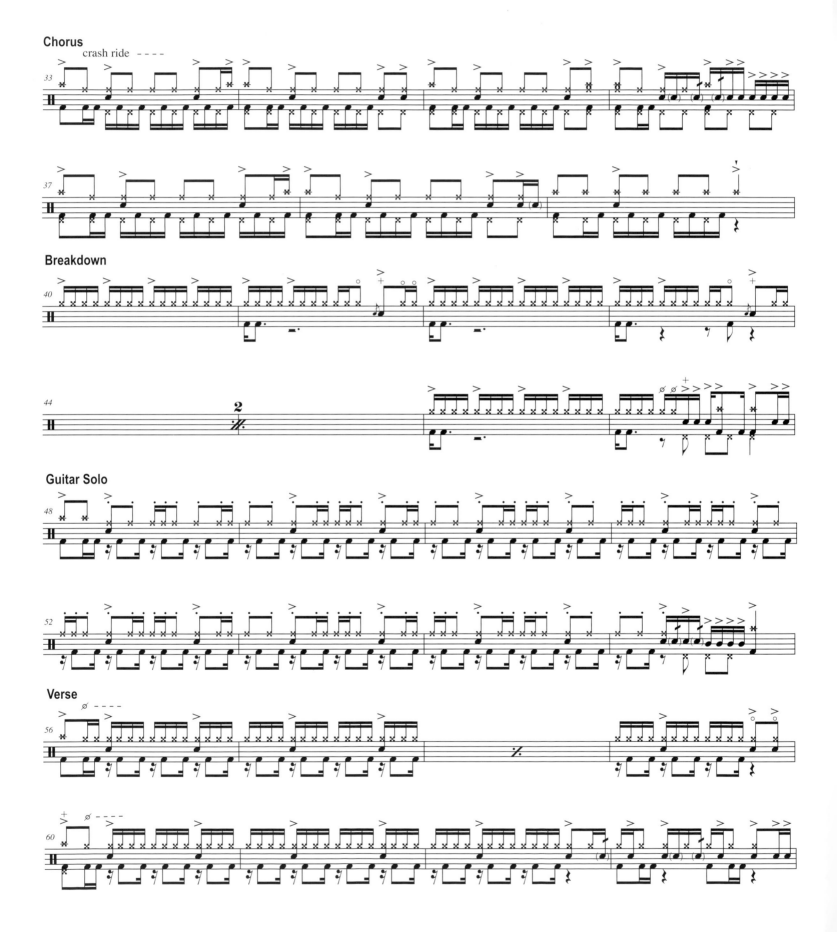

Breakdown

Guitar Solo

Verse

Chorus

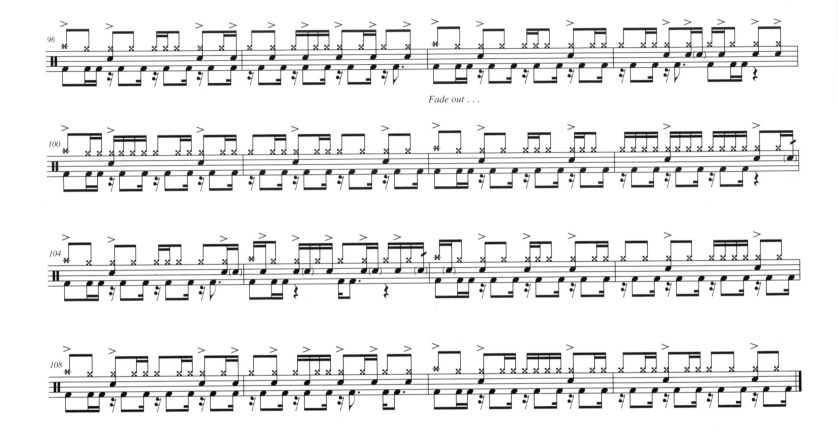

Fade out . . .

"I was a big fan of Tower of Power and that kind of music. Ed and I went everywhere and listened to everything. And whether it was your style of music or not, you had to appreciate the fact that what these guys are doing onstage is making the joint jump. Get the people out of their seats; get them participating; get them to enjoy the communal experience."

"Mine All Mine" (*OU812*)

Alex leads into a double-time groove over running double bass 16th notes on the intro of "Mine All Mine." The snare drum plays syncopated accents that work off of the keyboard rhythms.

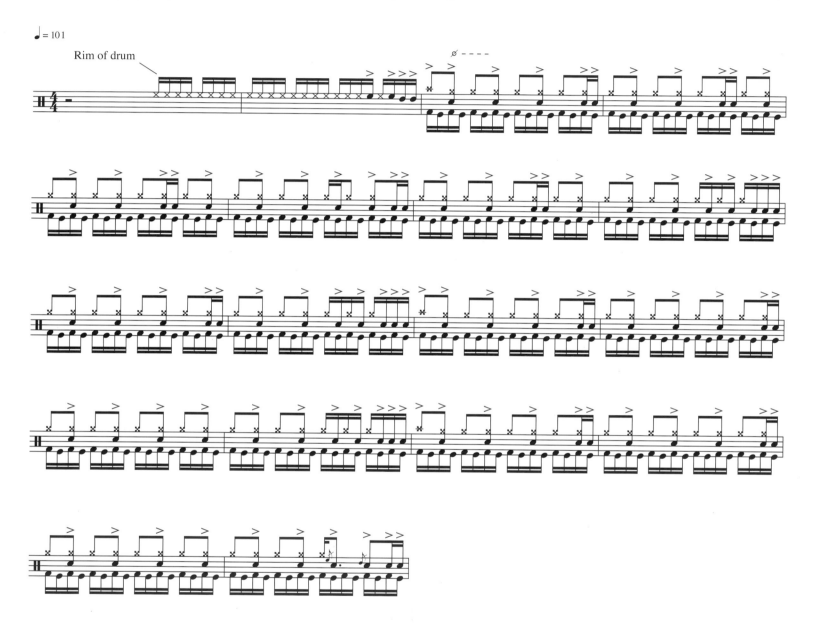

"Mine All Mine" continued

The section before the guitar solo features a slick cross-stick pattern that morphs into a double bass beat. The three-note groupings add tension at the end of the phrase.

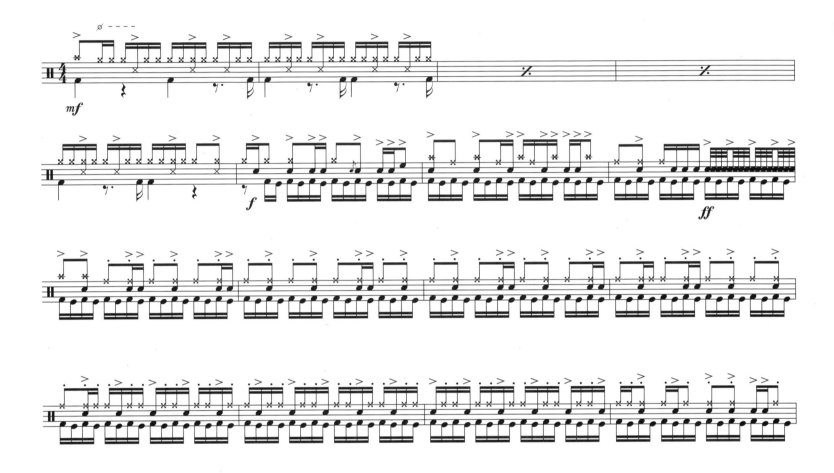

"Sometimes...I don't want to say the songs 'speak to you,' but it's pretty obvious to me what needs to be done to generate forward motion, just to keep it moving. Instinctively, you don't want to be locked in so tight that it sounds like everything's in unison. That's sterile and not human. Some people call it 'swing,' but you just need to loosen up and move the boundaries a little bit. Ultimately at the end of the take, if we liked it, that was a keeper. We didn't nitpick to try to get it perfect."

"Dirty Movies" (*Fair Warning*)

Alex lays down a smooth R&B 16th-note pocket groove à la Jeff Porcaro on "Dirty Movies."

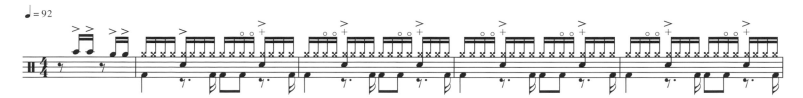

He plays a tom crescendo that is met with a double crash at the heavy guitar riff. He chokes the first crash, creating an effect that mimics the chorus vocals later in the song.

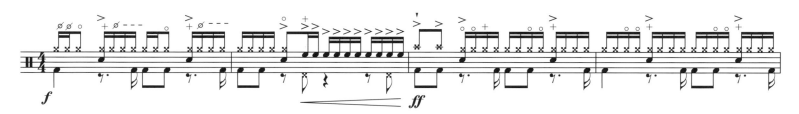

Alex sidesteps around the downbeats of the pre-chorus and pushes the accent over to the "and" of 1 to highlight the vocal phrasing.

Pre-Chorus

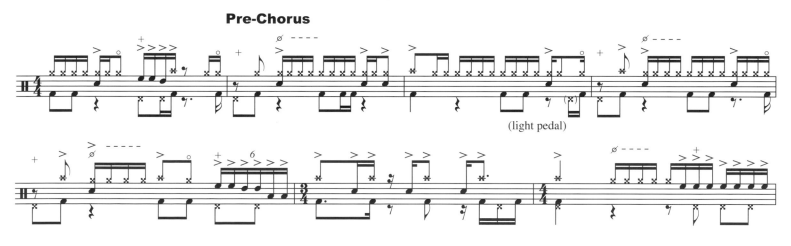

(light pedal)

Chorus

"Dirty Movies" continued

He plays with a Bonham-istic approach through the guitar interlude before the breakdown.

The hi-hat plays upbeats between the pedaled notes while the snare drum plays 16ths on the ending fill.

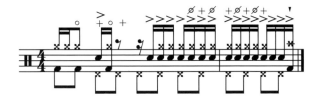

"Vaudeville meets burlesque."

"Drop Dead Legs" (1984)

The groove on "Drop Dead Legs" is augmented by some well-thought-out cymbal overdubs. Here he places a crash in the space of the guitar riff on the verse.

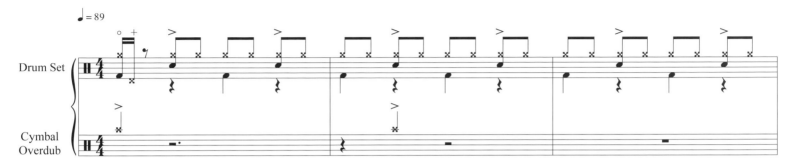

On the chorus, he adds 8th notes on the ride cymbal bell and accent crashes on top of the bass drum/snare/hi-hat beat.

"Drop Dead Legs" continued

He plays unison 16ths on the hi-hat and the overdubbed ride bell on the outro. The overdubbed hi-hat adds another layer of texture under the massive-sounding groove.

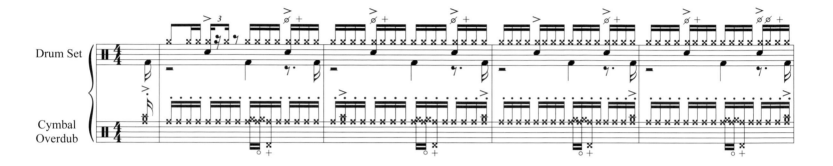

[Referring to the non-washy, tight hi-hat groove] "A lot of it is how you feel. There is no strong and fast rule. That was a lot of fun to record that. It was the first full record [1984] we did at Ed's studio. The process is just as interesting as anything. The outcome is almost secondary. You're not in there to make a record; you're in there to record what you're playing. It's a whole different mindset. You're not in there for an objective— you're in there because you love what you're doing, and it becomes recorded."

"5150" (5150)

"5150" is a great example of Alex's uptempo rock playing. There are lots of signature elements at work: the crash/ride in the chorus, the ride bell on the guitar turnarounds, the fully developed snare tone, as well as Simmons electronic sounds. The chorus can be deceiving, as the fills at the beginning of the measures lead into the "and" of beat 2. He turns up the heat near the end of the song with some fast double bass chops.

Verse

Pre-Chorus

Chorus

crash ride - - - -

Verse

stick click

(mute ride)

"5150" continued

Pre-Chorus

Chorus

crash ride - - - -

Guitar Solo

crash ride - - - -

"5150" continued

Fade out . . .

[Referring to the trademark washy ride work on choruses] "It depends on the texture of the song and whatever is going on around it. The cymbal wash came about, like with Keith Moon, when you're trying to fill some space. You've got the bass on the low end and a guitar on Mount Everest, so what are you going to do in the middle? So you fill it by riding on a swishy ride cymbal. It happens in three-piece bands. You can't just stick on the hi-hat. It's a sonic picture that we're painting. And there's a big hole in the middle, so put some paint in it!"

"Pleasure Dome" (*For Unlawful Carnal Knowledge*)

Alex starts the song "Pleasure Dome" with timbale-like solo fills across the toms. The double bass drums keep a galloping 8th/16th ostinato underneath.
Note: The bass drum pattern is notated right-foot lead, but other approaches can be applied. Experiment with what is most comfortable for you.

Alex plays alternating 16th notes in the verse with accents on counts 2 and the "e" of 4.

He plays quick ride-bell 16th-note rhythms on the chorus that add a Latin element to the groove.

This extended three-over-two phrase leads into the guitar solo.

"I wanted to do kind of a Latin thing. The beginning part was an homage to Ginger Baker without coming close to repeating one of his patterns. Nobody could do it better than the original. Some of the stuff is in your muscle memory, and it sneaks in when you're not thinking. But most of the time when you're playing, you're not thinking anyway. If you're thinking, the moment's already passed."

"Can't Get This Stuff No More" (Best Of, Vol. 1)

The hi-hat and guitar intro on "Can't Get This Stuff No More" can be elusive. Alex's African-influenced phrasing on the hi-hat floats through the barlines and resolves in unexpected places. After laying down a big fill, he launches into a bluesy 12/8 groove.

Alex mixes it up with a cowbell groove on the second verse.

The beat through the guitar solo sounds almost "backwards" as the bass drum and snare play an offbeat rhythm through the 12/8 meter. This is another great example of Alex's inspired creativity.

"You pay tribute to the guys before you, and that's very much a Ginger Baker thing. Very African. I have some old tapes of Ginger and Tony Allen. Granted, I didn't put the accent where it normally goes, which is on 2, which makes it lean the other way. But in the context of the song, that's how we played it."